Twists of Fate

A Journey Through Time

Jim Van De Veire

Vigilant Always—Batavia, IL
Paperback ISBN: 979-8-3305-8426-0
eBook ISBN: 979-8-3305-8463-5
Twists of Fate: A Journey Through Time
Author: Jim Van De Veire
Available formats: eBook | Paperback distribution

Published in the United States by New Book Authors Publishing

Dedication

iii

To my wife Cindy without whom
This journey through life would not have been possible.

Table of Contents

Preface

As we go through our lives, we seldom think about the collective choices that we make and how they might alter our lives and the lives of others. Everyone has had things happen in their lives which have changed their future. Some of these may have occurred long before they were even born. Others might have been decisions that you made, or choices you did not take. "If only I had done that" or "that could have been me," or any number of statements about alternatives to the decisions we did make. Our entire lives are a series of things that happen that we may or may not have control over. The truth is sometimes things happen, and we do not know why. Some people believe that things just happen by chance. Other people believe that there is some unknown higher power that guides us with the choices we make, and still others believe that God allows us to choose our own paths. In any case, no one ever makes the right choice every time. When we look back at our lives hopefully, we can say that we made the right choice most of the time.

This is my story about the twist and turns of fate that occurred before, and during my life that made me who I am today. I am hoping that anyone who reads this book will reflect on their own lives and think about the key things in their lives that made them the person that they are now. Remember, a single act can have ramifications beyond one's own comprehension, that impact not only on you, but on those around you.

Chapter 1
In a Land Long Ago

Most stories about the things that impact your life begin at one's birth, but in this case, my story begins over 300 years ago in the Duchy of Flanders. Flanders is the lowlands between Holland and what is now Belgium. Most of Flanders is composed of land that was reclaimed from the sea over the centuries. It is a land that was full of windmills that were used to pump the water back into the sea and dikes to keep the sea out of lowlands that had been created.

At the time, America had already been a British colony for 103 years and would still be a British colony for another fifty-seven years. Meanwhile in Flanders, the people were trying to recover from the Great Frost which occurred in the winter of 1709. Temperatures reached their lowest point in over four hundred years. By the end of 1710, the Great Frost was responsible for over 600,000 people perishing from famine and diseases due to the bitter cold and starvation. Over the centuries Flanders had been part of many countries dating back to the occupation of the Romans because of its strategic location between what are now France and Germany. In the early eighteen century Flanders was then a part of the Austrian Empire. The Empress Maria Theresa of Austria (1717-1780) was the ruler of Austria at the time. All the Netherlands was under Austrian control thru most of the early eighteen century. It started to change in 1740 when the War of Austrian Succession began. This war would last until 1748 with the signing of the Peace of Aix-la-Chappelle. The political chaos, the great famine, and the backlash from the Protestant

Reformation made for an exceedingly difficult life for the people of Flanders, especially the poorer classes. Flanders had been known for making fine woolen goods and linens in the fifteenth and sixteenth centuries, but many of those industries had moved out of the area because of the lack of political stability. The local people were often taxed by more than one country, each laying claim to Flanders. Over the years Austria, France, Spain, the Netherlands, and even England for a brief period had laid claim to Flanders. The people were also under tremendous religious pressure. The protestant reformation was in full switch, and every country who claimed Flanders was pressuring the citizens to convert to their preferred religion. Spain wanted the people of Flanders to remain Catholic. France wanted them to accept the Protestant religions during the reformation. In 1794 Napoleon would be the latest to take possession of Flanders, and it would become part of the Empire of France until Napoleon was defeated at the Battle of Waterloo in 1815. In 1815 Flanders would change hands again. Flanders was given to the Netherlands by the Congress of Vienna. The Dutch were now the newest country to control Flanders. Due to the continued unrest even more of the few remaining industries left Flanders. The weavers and most of the linen makers continued to relocate to more stable regions. Flanders had become primarily an area of small farms and just a few die-hard makers of fine linen products.

The unrest had made life more difficult for the poor people in Flanders. However, life had to go on and a young man named Joannes Van

Kaprijke City Hall

De Veire, a farmer by trade met a young lady in the village where they both lived. The village was called Sleidinge, and it was a part of the municipality of Evergem, which is located about ten kilometers (6.2 mi) northwest of Ghent, in what is now Belgium. The young lady's name was Joanna Pyckevet. The people in Belgium even to this day do not move far from their ancestral homes. Joannes Van De Veire was born in 1710, shortly after the Great Frost. He was about five foot five inches tall with dark hair and brown eyes. This was the average height for men in the early 18th century in Northwestern Europe. He was twenty-one-years-old when he and Joanna got married. They were married on February 19, 1732, in Sleidinge. They would go on to have five children together during their marriage of twenty years. On February 7, 1737, they would have their third child. It was their third boy. His name was to be Judocus. He was named after his grandfather on his mother's side. They would have two more children after Judocus. In all, they would have five children. All five children were boys. Joannes and Joanna would be my great, great, great, great, great, grandparents.

St. Egiduis Church in Lembeke

Judocus was also a farmer. When he grew up, he married another member of the Pyckevet family. Her name was Livina, and she was born on September 11, 1736. She was a year older than Judocus. They were married in the town of Oosteeklo on April 26, 1760, less than six miles from the village in which they were both born. They would have eleven children together over their forty-one years of marriage. Of their eleven children only six of the children would live to reach adulthood. Child mortality rates in Europe in the early 18th century were between thirty to forty percent. This was due to disease, poor sanitation conditions, and famine. Petrus would be the sixth child that Judocus and Livina would have together.

Petrus was born on April 17, 1770. Petrus grew up in the town of Sleidinge. He would eventually meet a woman from the neighboring town of Lovendegem. Her name was Christina De Backer. Christina was born on February 27, 1764. Christina and Petrus were married on May 13, 1794, in Sleidinge. Christina was thirty years old when they got married. They would only have three children during their marriage. I believe that Petrus died at a young age. There is no record of Petrus after 1804 when their last child was born. Of their three children two of them were boys. The youngest of their three children was a boy named Donatus.

Records in French Circa 1794

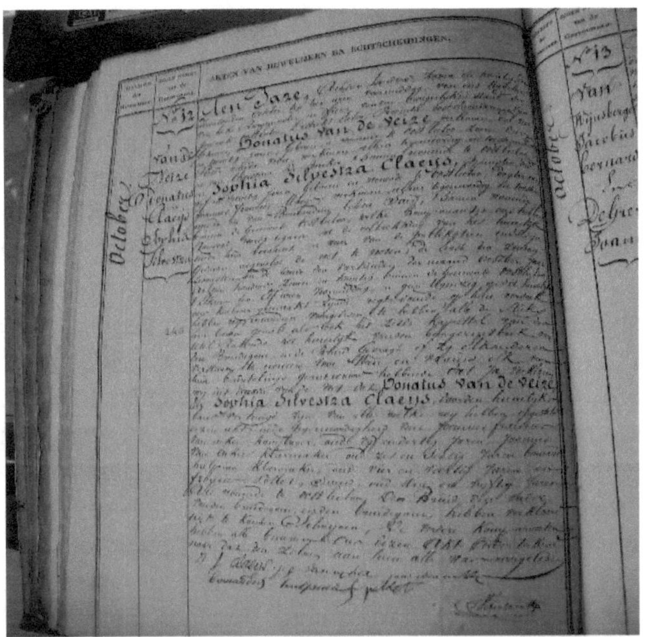

Records in Flemish Circa 1804 Birth of Donatus Van De Veire

Donatus was born on March 10, 1804, in the town of Assenede. He met Sophia Claeys when he was twenty-two years old. Sophia was just a few months older than Donatus when they met. She was born on August 31, 1803. Sophia and Donatus would get married when she was twenty-four on October 17, 1827. They were married at the city hall in Kaprijke. The city hall in Kaprijke is still in use today. They would have nine children together, four girls and five boys. During Donatus's life he was also a farmer. He would live to the ripe old age of eighty-six. He passed away on November 8, 1890, at his home in Oosteeko at 3 AM. Donatus would eventually be my great, great, grandfather. Sophia proceeded him in death. She died on September 6, 1879. Of the nine children, only two of the boys would grow up and have children of their own. One of the two boys would be named Joannes Baptiste. Joannes Baptiste Van De Veire was my great grandfather.

Joannes Baptiste was born on January 17, 1833, in the town of Oosteeko, Belgium. He was born shortly after the Belgium Rebellion which occurred in 1830. In this rebellion France had assisted the Belgium people, which included Flanders in securing their independence from the Netherlands. Leopold I was made king of the kingdom of Belgium in 1831. It took an addition eight years for the major powers to recognize Belgium as its own country. This recognition was part of the Treaty of London on April 19, 1839. The people of Flanders were now officially Belgian. Joannes would grow up to become a cattle merchant. I consider Joannes to be the first salesperson in the Van De Veire family. His job was to buy and sell small cattle herds. He would then take them to market to sell them collectively for all the neighboring farms. This would allow the farmers to secure a better price for their herds, and in some cases reduce the amount of taxes that were incurred by having a larger herd. Joannes met a young lady named Urgela De Roo. Urgela was the youngest of eight children in the Livinius De Roo family. She was born on August 6, 1833, in the village of Lembeke. Joannes and Urgela De Roo were married on February 20, 1863, in the town of Lembeke at 5 PM in St. Egiduis Church. They would have twelve children together. Six of the children were boys and six were girls. Unfortunately, only six of the twelve children lived to adulthood. Of the six children who died, four died in infancy. Joannes Baptiste passed away at the age of sixty-one on May 7, 1894, in Lembeke. Urgela, his widow lived a long life and died at the age of eighty-three on November 18, 1915. Urgela would live to see five of her six remaining children migrate to the United States. The youngest of the six surviving children was named Leo. Leo was born on May 8, 1879, in the town of Lembeke. He was baptized at St. Egiduis Church in the small town of Lembeke, as were all his siblings. Leo would eventually become my grandfather.

Conditions in Belgium in the late 1800s continued to be difficult for the Flemish speaking lower classes. Although they were now a separate kingdom they were still not treated equally. In fact, Flemish (Dutch) was not recognized as an official language for any legal documents at the time. Over the upper-class French speaking people held eighty percent of the government offices. Changes to the laws in Belgium were coming that would make life better for the Flemish speaking people and level the playing field with the French speaking upper class. However, change was not coming soon enough for three Van De Veire brothers. They were impatient for a better life and decided to seek their fortunes in the United States. The three brothers Louis (also called Charles), Ivo, and Leo migrated to the United States early in 1899 from Antwerp, Belgium to seek their fortune in the USA. Leo was the youngest of the three brothers, he was just nineteen at the time that they departed Belgium.

They arrive at Ellis Island after a 4-week long voyage across the Atlantic Ocean in third class on board the steamship Southwark on April 5, 1899. After going through an extensive stay in immigration at Ellis Island they continued their journey to Chicago, Illinois to start a business together. They had been told that Illinois was a good state to live in for people from Belgium. It was customary practice for the officials at Ellis Island to suggest places for different immigrates to go based on the area they came from in Europe. The brothers then traveled by train to Chicago. Their plan was to start a business in Chicago. Unfortunately. things did not work out with the three brothers and their business venture in Chicago. They all decided to leave Chicago and go their separate ways. Louis, the oldest of the three brothers, moved to South Bend, Indiana. Ivo, the middle of the three brothers moved to Grand Rapids, Michigan. Leo decided that he had seen enough of the United States and returned to Belgium. Leo's decision to return home to Belgium would have a tremendous effect on the future of the Van De Veire family.

Once Leo returned to Belgium from the United States, he remained there for eleven years. At some point after his return to Lembeke in Belgium he met a young lady named Emma Van Hecke. Emma was seven years his junior. She was born on June 29, 1886. She was the daughter of the local photographer in Lembeke. They start seeing each other and got married when she was just eighteen in 1904. They had two children while in Belgium. Their names were Julia born October 3, 1908, and Aime (Emil) who was born on December 16, 1906. A year after Julia was born, Leo, Emma, and their two children decided to immigrate to the USA. Once again Leo went through Ellis Island, except this time he was married with two children.

This second voyage was on board the steamship Kroonland. They arrived in the United States on October 27, 1909. After departing Ellis Island in New York for the second time, Leo, Emma, and their two children migrated to Illinois. They settled in Chicago and lived there for several years. Thet lived in a building on Harrison Street that is still standing today. Leo worked at a dairy while they lived in Chicago. In 1921 they moved to St. Charles, Illinois. A small town with an exceptionally large Belgium population at the time. In fact, the Belgium population in the town was so large, that the east side of town was called Belgium town. Leo worked as a night guard at the Lithograph Printing Company in St. Charles.

He and Emma would go on to have nine more Children while in the United States. Six of the additional children were girls and three were boys. Three of the girls died in childbirth. Their names were Ema, Zulma, and Mary Ellen. The remaining eight children, two of whom were born in Belgium all reached adulthood. The tenth child was a boy, and they would name him Harold Leo. He was born on May 5th, 1924. He was to become my father. He was eighteen years younger than his oldest sibling, Emil. Emma was forty years old when Harold was born. Thank goodness they decided they needed another boy!

Chapter 2
Chance Encounters

Ironically, a large part of my knowledge about my ancestors was one of the strangest twists of fate. Let's fast forward to the year 2009. One of my cousins received a strange phone call from woman in Missouri. She claimed to have found a man's wallet while taking a hike near her home in Missouri. In it there was a driver's license from Illinois that had the name Van De Veire on it with an address in Illinois. My guess is that my uncle had lost the wallet while traveling in the area. The woman who found the wallet immediately recognized the name as being Flemish. She and her mother had migrated to the United States from Belgium and settled in Missouri. Their last name was Van Hecke, and they were related to my grandmother Emma. The woman reached out my cousin and told her about the wallet she had found and how she knew the name from Belgium. My cousin called me and told me about what had happened, and she thought I might be interested in the information that she had from the relatives in Missouri. This got me started on finding out more information about the family. This led to my wife and I going to Belgium to the town of Lembeke where my ancestors were born.

The journey to Belgium was epic. We flew from Chicago to the city of Brussels in Belgium. We then took a train ride from Brussels to the city of Ghent. Next, we boarded a large city bus in Ghent to the town of Eeklo, Belgium. After that came a transfer to a small bus that went to the small town of Lembeke. When we arrived in Lembeke, we got off the bus and the first thing we saw was a World War I monument next to the bus stop. It was just in front of the St. Egiduis Catholic church. The first name on the monument was a Van De Veire, who was killed in WW1. At that point, I knew I was home! Once we arrived in Lembeke. We had to figure out where to go to find out more about my family. We started to walk around the small town looking for a place where we might find someone who could help us. We spotted an older man walking down the street carrying a black leather bag. It turned out he was a doctor, and he was making house calls! Fortunately, he spoke English, and he told us that records for Lembeke where now in the town of Kaprijke. As it turned Lembeke had lost its status as a town and been annexed into Kaprijke in 1975. We hailed a taxi and took a short ride to Kaprijke. We had the driver drop us off at the local church. Next to the church was a small cemetery. We figured that we could start at the local cemetery to see if we could find any information that would help us. My wife, who inherited the ability to talk to anyone from her mother, struck up a conversation with an older lady who had just arrived at the cemetery on her bicycle. The amazing part about this was that Cindy did not speak a word of Flemish.

After a few minutes, the older lady motioned for us to follow her. She walked her bike and us over to a nearby house. A conversation then ensued between herself and the lady of the house. The second woman then sent her husband off on his bicycle to get someone who spoke English. At least that is what we assumed. She told us to just wait on the porch.

A few minutes later the husband came back on his bicycle with another man, whose name was Roger Buyck. Roger was somewhat famous in the area. He is a published author and an expert on the history of the area. Roger then took us to the village hall. Unfortunately, it was not open for visitors at the time. Roger somehow got us access into the city hall and down to the old archives. They were leather bound and written in either French or Flemish depending on the dates. In these records were many of the detail that formed a large part of the research of my family in Belgium. If Cindy had not started the conversation with the women in the cemetery, we might never have gotten the first-hand information on my family. This entire sequence was a series of twists and turns that led me down the right path to find the origin of my story. It all started with a chance encounter several thousands of miles away from Flanders.

Let us recap our journey to the past thus far. We have gone back over 214 years, through seven generations and fifty-one children to get to Harold, my father. If any one of my ancestors had made a choice that was different in those 214 years, they would have altered the future generations. Joannes and Urgela might have never met, and Leo would not have been born and migrated to the United States not once but twice. He would not have married Emma, and my father would not have been born. This would be the end of my story before it began.

S.S. Southward arriving Ellis Island

SS Kroonland

Leo & Emma 1899

Chapter 3
World War II

In December 7th, 1941, the Japanese attack Pearl Harbor without warning or provocation. All American was outraged, President Franklin Roosevelt call it a "day of infamy" and declared war on Japan. Young men all over the country rushed to enlist in one of the military services. In 1942, Harold enlisted in the Navy. One of his older brothers, Albert, had enlisted about a year earlier in the Navy.

When enlisting during WWII in the Navy, you had the option to sign up for six years or the duration of the War. My father decided that six years was the best option for him. He expected that the war would last longer than six years. This choice would greatly impact his future and mine.

After completing basic training at Great Lakes Naval Training Center, he was assigned to a Navy cruiser. Her name was the USS Mobile, official designation CL-63. The Mobile had just been commissioned on March 24, 1943. During her time in WWII, she participated in over thirty battles and shot down fifteen Japanese planes and sank six ships. On November 20th, 1944, an event occurred in Ulithi, in the Carolina Islands that could have dramatically impacted my history. Two Japanese submarines attacked the USS Missisinewa, a tanker, and the USS Mobile, both ships were stationary at the time. The tanker was hit by a torpedo from one of the subs and heavily damaged and sunk. The second sub targeted the USS Mobile. A torpedo was fired at pointblank range but failed to detonate. The hit was in the middle of the ship and if it had exploded, many of the crew of the Mobile would not have survived. My father was part of the

Damage Control team, which had their repair shop midship. If it had exploded, my father would probably not have survived the torpedo hit, and my story would never have begun. Fate had intervened to save the men of the USS Mobile. I am sure that God had greater things for the members of this crew to accomplish in the future. Others would say that it was just not their time or that it was just a lucky break.

USS Mobile (CL-63)

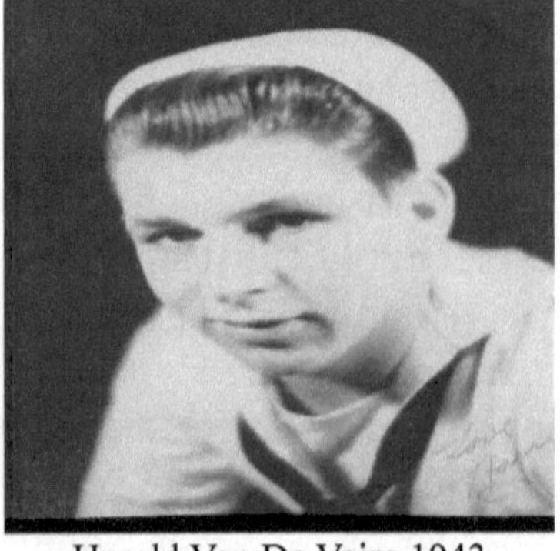

Harold Van De Veire 1943

My father stayed with the USS Mobile from when she was commissioned on March 24th, 1943, until she was decommissioned in 1948. She was placed on active duty at the Naval Shipyard in Portsmouth, Virginia. Her final voyage was to Seattle, Washington where she was to be scrapped in 1948. After his honorable discharge from the Navy as a Petty Officer 2nd class, he returned to his home in St. Charles, Illinois. Unfortunately, on his trip back home from Washington, the used car he had bought was broken into and everything he owned was stolen, except for a box containing his roller skates and the clothes he had on his back. Apparently, the thief was either not a skater or had small feet!

As with many of those returning from service after World War II, he needed to get a job. He decided to learn a trade. My father had not graduated from high school, so he felt that what he had learned in the Navy as a ship fitter would help him find a job. He initially started out as an apprentice carpenter but changed to the trade of brick and stone mason. He told me he made the change because at the time brick masons made more money than carpenters.

Chapter 4
The First Time

My father's favorite past times were skating and bowling, but the nearest roller rink at the time was in Glen Ellyn, Illinois about 20 miles from St. Charles. He regularly went skating at that rink. Sometime, in early 1949 he had a chance meeting with a girl from Angel Guardian orphanage in Chicago. She and two of her girlfriends had just finished their time at the orphanage. You had to leave the orphanage when you were eighteen years old. They had decided to go roller skating in Glen Ellyn because one of the girls she was with had a boyfriend near Glen Ellyn. The young woman he met had jet black hair and was short. She was four feet eleven inches tall with brown eyes. Her name was Madeline Ann Marchese, and she was the youngest of three children. She had an older sister named Connie and an older brother named Carlo. Both of whom had left the orphanage earlier. Their mother had died when Madeline was two years old and my grandfather Rocco, could not support the three children so he put them in the care of the orphanage. This was a quite frequent practice among poor catholic immigrants in the 1920's.

As it turns out Madeline was new to skating but wanted to learn. My father was a particularly good skater and offered to help her learn to skate. He thought that as short as she was even if she fell, she would not have far to fall. They hit it off very well, and over the next few months, they met to go skating. In fact, they went so often that my mother bought her own skates. After dating for a few months, they got engaged and then married in 1950. If my father had not decided to select the six-year option when he enlisted in the Navy, he would not have been at that roller rink that day when Madeline was there. This chance meeting of two people would never have occurred. The orphanage and my father's home in St. Charles are over sixty miles apart. Their separate decisions to go to the roller rink that specific day had made their meeting possible, or was it fate that had once again stepped in.

Madeline and Harold's Wedding

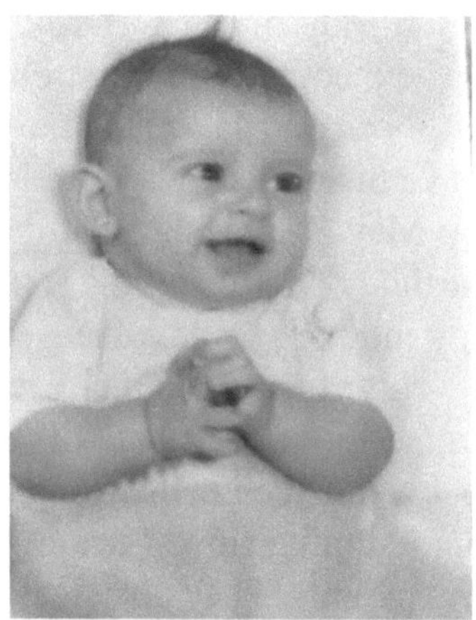

The New Baby (Jim)

Chapter 5
The Early Years

In May of 1951 Harold and Madeline Van De Veire were expecting their first child. The child was supposed to be born on May 5th, but my future mother wanted the child to have his or her own birthday, so she decided to have the baby on May 7th. My father thought to would be cool to have my birthday and his on the same date, but as in most cases where my mother was involved, she got her own way.

This change of date would have a major impact on my life in the future, but that will be in another chapter. I was a small baby, nineteen inches long and 6 lb. 7 oz. Which was probably a good thing since I was a breach baby. I was the first child for my parents. They also decided to name me Jim and not James, this would cause me much grief with the nuns when I went to Catholic school. They had a baby two year later who was named Richard, but he died in the first week of his life. Three years after Richard had passed away my parents had my brother Robert, and three years after that they had my little sister, Barbra Ann. My parents told me once that they only wanted three children, so based on what they had told me, my sister would never have been born if Richard had lived. This of course would have been the end of her story.

Being born in the fifties, things were a lot different from how children are raised now. We had a lot more freedom as to what we could do alone. Our parents allowed us to go play outside until it was dark, and never thought that something bad could happen to us. The list of things that we "survived" comes up regularly on Facebook, so I will only list a few. We drank water from the garden hoses. We rode in the back of open pickup trucks. We rode in cars with no seat belts, sometimes even in the front seat! We even took public transportation on our own. However, the most important thing was we had to talk to people, and if we were going to criticize someone, we had to do it in person. We could not hide behind some social media online to comment on something we liked or did not like. Based on what is accepted as normal now, it is a miracle that any of us have reached adulthood. In my case not only was I the oldest child in our family, but I was also the only child for about three years within my parent's circle of friends. So, you could say that I was doted on by all their friends, but I would say that I was just ahead of my time.

One of my first memories of things that I did that were unusual occurred when I was four years old. We rented the upstairs of a house on Grace Street in Elgin Illinois. They rented it from our milkman at the time, who was a close friend of theirs. It was the only place that my parents could afford. My parents had a 1946 blue chevy coupe with a three speed on the column. We had to park it on the street because we did not have a driveway or a garage. Grace Street is located on a steep hill which dead ends with Bluff City Boulevard. At the bottom of the hill was a furniture store called Rauschenberger. I decided to go out and play in the car. I pretended that I was a race car driver and put the gear shift stick into neutral. The car started rolling backwards down the hill. My father saw the car moving and came running out towards me, but the car was moving too fast. It rolled about thirty feet backwards and was picking up speed. Then suddenly it stopped. I had left the door open when I was racing, and the door caught on a telephone pole and stopped the car. If I had closed the door I would have rolled down into traffic or worse into the showroom of the furniture store. I may have set the record for the youngest driver to have a car accident, but I neglected to have it submitted to Guinness Book of Records at the time. Once my father caught up with car. He pulled me out and told me to sit on the curb. He then drove the car back up to its original location, parked it and locked it this time. I cannot remember what my punishment was, but my father said something to me in Flemish, and I do not think it was a complement. The look he gave me was enough punishment. I do remember that I fell in love with cars that day. I had learned about the need for speed!

My mother used to tell everyone about the first time I met Santa Claus, I was five at the time. She took me with her to go shopping at Joseph Spiess Company in Elgin. It was a high-end department store. My mother had expensive taste even though we did not have a lot of money. In fact, she had her own personal shopper at Spiess. The shoppers were called Mrs. Page. I am assuming that was not her real name. I stood in line with the other kids to meet Santa, and when I finally got to my turn to sit on Santa's lap. He gave me a small truck as a gift. I looked at it and turned around and told Santa, I wanted a big truck. Both lady elves tried not to laugh, and Santa just rolled his eyes. I left with the small truck, but it was clear that even as a child I liked to think. My mother grabbed me by the arm and dragged me out of the store. I learned to speak my mind exceedingly early; it was one of the traits I inherited from my mother. Fortunately, in my later life my wife taught me to think about what I was going to say before I said it.

My first real test of freedom was when I was in kindergarten. We lived about four blocks away from Huff School in Elgin. I had to walk to school every day alone, can you imagine letting a five-year-old child walk to school alone now days. Fortunately, nothing bad happened on these daily treks to school. My worst crisis happened one winter when we had extremely deep snow. I made it across both the busy streets enroute to school but got stuck in the deep snow that I had to cross in the field leading up to the school. When you are only a little over three feet tall, and the snow is over two feet deep you have a problem. I turned around and headed back to my house and told my parents that I could not walk across the field. My dad came to the rescue. He was off work that day because as a bricklayer they could not lay brick if it was below freezing. So, he walked with me to the field and then picked me up and carried me the rest of the way to school. Thank goodness I went home and did not try to go alone. I could have ended up as a story in the newspaper about a child who froze to death four blocks from their home.

Other than the deep snow incident, I enjoyed the walk to kindergarten every day. On my route back from kindergarten I would stop at the Cornish Sisters' house. They were two older ladies, who ran a candy shop. It was like Fanny May, except their shop was in their basement. I would get a free piece of candy every day! I am glad that I did not get baked in one of their ovens like in the fairy tale.

After kindergarten, I attended grades 1-4 at St. Joseph School in Elgin. I was the smallest kid in the class, including the girls. This led to me always being in the front of the line for everything, so it was hard for me to get away with anything. At St. Joseph school we had annual plays, and because of my diminutive size, I ended up playing whatever the smallest character was in the play. I remember being a rabbit, a frog, a page, and even a fairy in different plays. This is why I was never worried about looking foolish, or it could have been something I inherited from my father. I was told that if there was a party and someone had a lampshade on their head, it would be my father, and he would be the sober one!

Most of our teachers were nuns, but we did have a couple of lay teachers. Again, it was the fifties and corporal punishment was common. Some of the teachers were more hands-on than others. One of the memorable incidents occurred during lunch one day. I was probably acting up too much when Miss Mc Keever grabbed me by the back of the neck, and she had fingernails! She had to bend over to grab me. I had a My Friend Flicka lunchbox with a full thermos in my hand at the time. I swung it around and caught the teacher in the head and knocked her out! The rest of my day did not go well, I got expelled from school for a week. My parents did not give me any additional punishment. This was probably because of the marks on my neck! However, when I returned to school, I was the hit of the class. (pun intended) This was my first brush with fame, even if it was of the notorious type!

During my first four years of grades 1-4, I traveled by public bus to various places in Elgin. For example, I attended swimming lessons which involved a transfer of two buses to get to the other side of town. This is when I had my first encounter with an overzealous swimming instructor. She decided that the best way to learn how to swim was to have the student simply jump in the deep end and start swimming. I advised her that I did not think I could do it, but she decided that I could. I jumped in and sank like a rock in twelve feet of water. It seemed like I was under water for a long time before the instructor jumped in and pulled me out of the water and got me breathing again. I reminded her that I told her that I could not swim. That was my last swimming lesson.

The swimming incident triggered another adventure. Since I decided that I was not going to continue swimming lessons. I did not think I should tell my mother. I decided to run away from home instead. I was in third grade at the time, and I just started walking. I left our house on the south side of Elgin, Illinois, and started walking north towards Carpentersville, Illinois. I am not sure why I went in that direction, but it seemed like a clever idea at time. I walked for just over five and half miles and then sat down in a gas station that was under construction. This is where I intended to spend the night, but after about 30 minutes of sitting in the gas station on a bale of hay, I elected to walk back home. In all I walked about eleven miles total. I did not get caught and no one offered to give me a ride. When I got home, I told my parents that I was not going to continue swimming lessons. I am sure that they suspected something, but they never said anything about it. They were fine with my decision to quit swimming lessons. I still wonder how I walked that far without being picked up by someone. My running away could have ended very badly. I am now over seventy years old, and I still cannot swim!

Chapter 6
Movin on Up

When I was in 5th grade, we moved to St. Charles, Illinois from Elgin, Illinois. My father and mother did not have much money. My Dads work as a bricklayer was sometimes seasonal and my mother was a part time waitress. They did not have enough money to buy a house that was already built. So, my father, having been a carpenter and now a bricklayer, knew he could build a house far less expensive than if they bought one that was already built. It took him over five years of work on the weekends to get it to the point that we could move into it. When we did move into our new house in St. Charles, it was still not finished but it had passed the inspection required for residency. It was an interesting house to live in to say the least. Most of the floors were tar papered because the flooring was not down yet, and the only interior door on the house was in the one bathroom we had at the time. The new house was located near my father's older brother's house, so we regularly went with him when he worked on the house. This was the first and only home that my parents owned during their lifetime.

My uncle Al was a big fisherman and hunter. He tried to get my father into fishing, but it did not seem like he had much interest in that area. He did, however, take to hunting and wanted to get me involved with the sport. When I was eleven years old, I got a 20-gauge single shot shotgun for Christmas. It was designed smaller than what would have been used by an adult. I was excited to try it out, so my father took me pheasant hunting. We were out hunting in a big field along the railroad tracks, and I was not paying much attention to the tracks because I was looking for birds. My foot slipped and got caught between the outside rail and the third rail on the tracks, and I could not get it free. This would not have been important except the third rail was electrified and a train was coming. My Dad saw that I was caught and ran back to where I was stuck. He yanked me out of my boot and off the train track just as the train went zooming past. This could have been the end of my story, if not for my dad's quick reaction, which saved my life. This would not be the last time my dad saved my life.

One day at the weekend, we went for a ride in my parents' 1954 Pontiac Chieftain. This was in 1961, and my parents had never owned a new car until 1970 after I had left home. The goal was to check out some more of the Fox Valley. With my dad and mom working most weekends we did not have a lot of free time just to go for a ride. Our big move from Elgin to St. Charles the previous year was only ten miles driving distance. To me it seemed like we were going to another world. We started driving out towards North Aurora, Illinois when we drove by a big high school campus. There was a monumental sign at the entrance that said MARMION. I asked my parents what kind of school it was, and they told me that it was a Military High School that was part of the Junior Reserve Officers Training Course (JROTC). I immediately told my parents that I was going to go to school there. My mother said, "We can't afford to send you to a school like that."

My mother did not understand the concept of having a positive attitude. I resolutely told them again that I was going to go there. I was eleven years old at the time. Two years later I got a job as a dishwasher at a local bar/restaurant called the "Y" Owl, where my mother was a waitress. I worked there on Friday and Saturday nights. I was paid a dollar an hour and worked fourteen hours a week. Over the next two years I saved up enough money to pay for my tuition and books for the first year at Marmion. It was a whopping $165 per semester. Now all I had to do was graduate from eighth grade and pass the entrance exam to attend Marmion. I took the exam in eighth grade and was one of four boys from St. Patrick's School that were accepted to attend the school. This was when I learned that if you wanted something bad enough and worked for it you could accomplish anything. My attending Marmion was a wise decision on my part. Later in life, I received an unexpected benefit for attending Marmion that would impact my adult life dramatically.

Entrance to Marmion Academy

Lake Street Campus

The school that I would go to before Marmion was St. Patrick's Catholic grade school. My early school St. Joseph in Elgin was also a Catholic School. The difference was at St Pat's you had to wear a school uniform. For the next 15 years of my life, I wore a green uniform of some sort. To this day, green is still my least favorite color. As you can imagine being the new kid in the school is never a lot of fun. Cyber-bullying did not exist yet. If you were going to bully someone you had to do it in person! Not only was I small for my age, but I was also not very coordinated, I made for the perfect target. This led to me not being picked to participate in baseball at lunch or after school with the cool kids. After a few weeks I got tired of not being selected so I started my own baseball game with all the kids who were not a part of the "cool kids" games. It turned out to be a big hit with everyone. Eventually, a lot of the cool kids decided to join in the games I had started. This was my first bona fide experience of being a leader, and I really liked it!

Apparently, the Nuns had taken notice of my initiative, and

they put me in charge of the patrol boys and gave me the rank of captain. We made sure that all the younger children got safely across the streets near the school and onto the correct buses. My job was to make sure that all the intersections and buses were covered by one of my team members and that they were on time and wearing patrol belts. This was before adult crossing guards who got paid to do the same thing. I did this for two years and loved being in charge. I learned a lot about responsibility and how to supervise other kids. Since all of this occurred after school, I usually could not catch the regular bus at grade school that took students over to the high school to catch another bus to their homes. I ended up walking to the high school or walking home from school. It was only a few blocks to the high school, but it was about four miles to our house. It was a great walk. I had to go past the local McDonalds, and since I was a working man, I would get shake, burger, and fries for a dollar or one hour of my pay. I always looked forward to these walks. Sometimes my uncle who lived across the street from us would see me walking and ask me if I wanted to ride in the back of his old blue Chevy pickup. Naturally, I would always accept, after all, what could be more exciting for a little boy than riding in the back of a truck as it barreled down an old country road. Who needs seat belts or even seats when you are thirteen or fourteen years old? It is funny to look back at the things we did as children that would be unheard of in today's normal modern family. Of course, that is assuming that I came from a normal family at the time.

In seventh grade I was thirteen years old and had my first encounter with death. My aunt Ruth had been killed in a car accident on April 1, 1964. Her car was struck by a person speeding and the car was split in half. Shortly after her passing, I was informed that I would be one of the pallbearers. At first, I was excited that I had been asked to participate in the arrangements like the older people. I knew nothing about funerals, so I had to ask what I had to do at the funeral. I was told that I would be one of six people who would carry the coffin into the church. Once I understood the scope of my role in the funeral,

I was petrified. I thought about what happens if I drop the coffin, or trip and fall. Fortunately, nothing went wrong in carrying the casket, but to this day I cannot look at a body that is in an open casket at a funeral. I think I was too young to be a pallbearer. I hoped that I would never have to be a pallbearer again, but in 1978 I had to serve as a pallbearer one more time. This time was even worse. My next-door neighbor and his family were on vacation in Kentucky Lakes and their three-year-old daughter somehow went into the water by herself. When Charlie looked around and saw that she was missing they started looking everywhere for her. She had fallen into the water off the dock and hit her head. The waves in the lake carried her under the dock and she drowned. When they brought her back to Illinois Charlie asked me to be a pallbearer. I could not refuse. It was one of the saddest things I ever had to do. The casket was so small that it only needed four pallbearers. I have not been asked to be a pallbearer since then nor do I plan to accept if asked.

On a less morbid note, later, that same year, we had a science fair at St. Patrick's School. Everyone was supposed to create their own project. I decided to construct a working old well. My father helped me with designing and building the oil well, but when it got to making it work, he thought it would be best if he did the soldering of the drill bit to the shaft of the motor. My plan was to have it be a small battery powered motor that would turn the drill bit like it was drilling into the ground. I thought this is going to be a sure "A" grade at the fair. Who else would be building a working oil well? The derrick itself looked great. I had built it myself entirely of wood. It stood about three feet tall. With the oil derrick now completed, all we had to do was attach the bit to the drive shaft of the motor. I had picked up some small copper tubes out of an old abandon barn about a half mile from our house. We thought that these caps would be perfect for selling the two items together. They seemed like innocent copper tubes that were closed at one end and about ¼" in diameter. They were a perfect fit for the end of our drill bit.

I held the motor in place while my father soldered the copper tube to the drill bit. I had to stand because the work bench was too high for me to sit and hold the motor. Everything was going smoothly until the solder hit the bottom of the copper tube. There was a huge explosion. It turns out the copper tubes were some type of blasting caps. The tube exploded and pieces of copper, solder, and metal went flying everywhere. My father ended up getting hit with pieces of shrapnel across his stomach. His T-shirt was now full of holes and blood was coming out of all the holes in his shirt. Due to our differences in height, I ended up with shrapnel up and down my left arm and across the upper part of my chest.

My father, my brother, and I

There was blood everywhere. My father grabbed some towels and wrapped up my arm and chest to stop the bleeding. He was also bleeding from his arm and stomach. Since my dad worked outside most of the time as a bricklayer, he had much tougher skin than a skinny seventh grader, so he did not seem to be bleeding as badly as I was.

My mother heard the explosion upstairs and ran to the top of the basement stairs to see what had happened. She then yelled these famous words that I still remember to this day. She said, "Jesus Christ, I thought the furnace blew up."

My mother was an enigma. She was this small Italian lady, who came across as quiet when you first got to know her, but that was not her real personality. She would offer her opinion on everything and was not really concerned about being politically or socially correct. I inherited that feature from her, but thanks to my wonderful future wife I have learned to keep it under control, most of the time.

My cousin Mike, who lived across the road, drove us to the hospital emergency room and they started picking the pieces out of all the holes in us. I do not remember the exact number that they got out that day, but I think it was about thirty pieces. For years afterwards, small pieces of metal would come to the surface, and we would pick them out. One of the pieces that was about the size of a pencil eraser tip struck me in the right eye. The good news is that I must have blinked at the right instant, and the piece of shrapnel embedded itself in my eye lid instead of my eye. To add insult to injury, I was given Penicillin for some reason, and we found out that I was allergic to it. I was quite the sight. My left arm is wrapped up in bandages from my hand to my upper arm. Another bandage wrapped around my chest. And both of my eyes swelled up from the Penicillin allergy. The most important thing was that I had not lost an eye. If I had lost my eyesight in one eye, it would not have been able to pursue a military career, and my entire future would have been altered.

The worst part of this was my teacher did not even give me an A on the project. I guess all the bloodshed did not impact her opinion of the project. She gave me a C on the project. In discussing it with my brother, he suggested that I should have changed the title of project to "An Oil Well Disasters," and that might have improved the grade.

My little brother Bob was not with us when we had the oil well disaster. If my little brother had been with us, he would have gotten the blast in the face, and there would be no telling what impact it would have had on him and his future. It surely would have impacted his story.

Chapter 7

It's not Easy Being Green

As I mentioned earlier, I told my parents that I would be going to Marmion and in 1965 I started my freshman year there. Marmion Military Academy was a nationally ranked honor military school. It was considered JROTC (Junior Reserve Officers Training Course) training. This meant that they were allowed to award a scholarship to West Point each year. Since I was an average student, a scholarship was not in my future. However, the training would come in handy in my later life and impact my future military service.

Marmion was divided into two campuses at the time. One was a daytime school, and the other was a boarding school. I attended daytime school. I learned later that the two campuses were combined three years after I graduated. Those of us who attended the Lake Street Campus were called "day beggars" by the other campus, and we called the rich kids at the Butterfield Road Campus "border rats." It cost several thousand to attend the boarding school, so that was out of my reach. I paid for all my tuition and books. The tuition and books for the day school in 1965 was about $330.00 per year, and of course it went up every year. I ended up quitting my job and the restaurant when I was sixteen because I could now work at other places legally. I ended up working two gas station jobs so that I could keep up with Marmion expenses. Fortunately, I was able to make enough money each year to pay for my four years at Marmion. Although I was resentful of my parents' inability to pay for my schooling, I did learn early in life the value of money. Paying my own way through high school I graduated from Marmion as a staff sergeant and member of the drill team in 1969. I was an average student while at Marmion. I made the honor roll a few times, but overall, I was a "B" student. My best grades were in Military Studies and my worst grades were in Latin. Thankfully, I did not run into any ancient Romans in my later life where that came into play. It was extremely helpful in reading the inscriptions on statues when I was in Europe later in life.

Senior Picture 1969   Basic Training 1970

After graduation in 1969 (left), I decided that I was not ready to attend college. I did not have any scholarship offers so I could not afford it anyway. My parents did not push me to go to college. I do not know if it would have made any difference as to whether I would go to college or not. In fact, I was surprised that I made it through my 18th year. Having this newfound freedom of not having to go to school and no plans for my future. It was my time to go crazy and do stupid things. I had my driver's license suspended for numerous speeding tickets in my GTO, but fortunately, I was able to hire a good lawyer, who got everything reduced so that I did not end up with a criminal record of any sort. If I had ended up being convicted, I am sure that it would have made it difficult if not impossible for me to join the military. I am still amazed that I made it through my eighteenth year with all the stupid things that I did. Looking back, I am confident that God had a plan for me.

Chapter 8

You're in the Army Now

In 1970, the Vietnam war was still going on and the United States required all males who were 18 years old to register for the draft. The Selective Service System conducted the draft to determine who was chosen for service. The lottery was based on your date of birth. This lottery system was in place from 1970 through 1975. The first lottery was conducted in July of 1969. This lottery would determine the numbers for the calendar year 1970. I was in the second lottery, which was held on July 1, 1970. The highest number selected for the calendar year 1971 was 125. As I mentioned earlier, I was supposed to be born on May 5th. If that had occurred, my lottery number would have been 301. So, I would not have had to go into the military. So that raises the question what was the lottery number for May 7, 1951? That lucky draft lottery number was 29. My entire military future was impacted by my mother deciding I should have my own birthday! Looking at it in retrospect I am glad it went the way it did, but at the time I was not happy. If I had told the recruiters I was supposed to be born two days earlier, I am sure they would have laughed and suggested a psychological evaluation.

I had no doubt that I would go into the service. The question was simply would I be drafted, or would I enlist? I decided that I would enlist so that I might at least have a chance of choosing where I might go, or what I might choose for skill specialty. I ruled out the Navy and the Coast Guard because I still could not swim, and I knew that would be a requirement for those two branches. I knew the Marines were not for me, so that left the Army and the Air Force as my two options. I picked the Army since I thought my background at Marmion would help me. This was another decision that ended up altering my future.

I went down to the recruiting station in Chicago and took a set of tests to determine what I was most qualified to do in the service. The Army decided that my best aptitude would be in one of the Quartermaster schools. They gave me a list of schools that I could attend, and Stock Control and Accounting (76P20) sounded interesting to me. I thought accounting would be handy when I got out of the Army. I would eventually go to Quartermaster school, but first eight weeks of basic training at Fort Lewis, Washington.

I began my military journey on August 20, 1970. I got to take the first airplane flight of my life! I was given a large manila envelope with my orders and a ticket to Tacoma, and I was on my way to a new adventure. Now when I see young people at O'Hare Airport with those same manila envelopes some fifty years later, I cannot help but smile. I hope that they will have some great adventures and stay safe as they begin their voyage like mine. Next, we were told in advance not to pack any luggage, just a shaving kit of some sort as the Army would provide us with everything else, we needed for basic training. A green army bus picked us up at Tacoma airport and took us to the base. The ride over was uneventful, it was raining. I found out later that it rained a lot in Washington. They even had shirts that said people in Washington do not tan, they rust. We then had ten days of orientation where we were given our uniforms and bedding before we started our basic training. If you have ever seen the movie Stripes, it has a sequence in it that covers the first few days in the Army. My first few days were exactly like the movie. We were lined up and marched off to receive our military gear. We were handed large green duffle bags, and given two sets of fatigues, two dress uniforms, boots, shoes, and assorted undergarments. We then left the quartermaster store, and we had everything we were going to need for clothing for the next ten weeks. Then it was off to the barracks to put things away and get in the fatigue uniform for our next adventure. The next adventure consisted of haircuts and then shots. Vaccinations were interesting because air guns for injections were extremely popular at the time. We were told to remain perfectly still while we got the shots. A couple of people moved, and the vaccination became a cut that bled quite a bit. This of course caused a couple of the people in line to pass out. Let us hope that those who passed out will not end up with jobs in which they saw a lot of blood later in their Army service. We each received a little yellow book that looked like a passport to keep track of our injections. These were our shot records, which we were told to keep with us whenever we visited one of the doctors. Little did I know that this book would eventually get filled up with various shots as I went to various locations. We were also given boxes to send any civilian clothes we had back to our homes. We were not allowed off base during basic training so there was no need for civilian clothes.

Little did I know how big an impact my decision to go to Marmion when I was twelve years old would have on my future. A few days after our time at the reception station, I learned that I was to start my time in service as a private E-2. I immediately started one rank higher than others who started out as private E-1. An E-2 was still private, but that usually took four months in service to attain. The second benefit came up as soon as I arrived at Fort Lewis, Washington when the Drill Sergeant (DI) asked if anyone had experience in Reserve Officers Training Course (ROTC). I raised my hand, which I learned later that you never do in the service. The Drill Instructor decided that he would make me the Platoon Guide, based on my having some Junior Reserve Officer Training Courses (JROTC) background. I was given snap-on Staff Sergeant stripes and was responsible for making sure that everyone was where they were supposed to be on time and properly dressed. He also told me to select four soldiers to be my squad leaders. They would wear Sergeant stripes. Since I am not a big guy, I decided the right course was to sign up the four biggest, meanest looking individuals in the platoon to be my squad leaders. It was easy to convince the four men I targeted to be Sergeants. There were a few perks for the position. The Platoon Guide and the Squad Leaders had their own room. Being in a room of just four other people was much better than been in an exceptionally large bay with thirty-two men. The barracks were all built in World War Two to house troops at that time who were preparing to go overseas to the Pacific Theater. They were meant to be temporary but were still in use in 1970.

Barracks from WWII still being used in 1970 at Fort Lewis Washington

My selection of the four Sergeants turned out to be a good strategy over the two months we were in basic training. Everyone did what they were supposed to do, and we did not have any serious issues. We only had one soldier out of our platoon who got recycled and had to go through basics again. This was the worst fate you could have, was to be recycled, because no one wanted to go through basics again. What most people do not realize is how bad the pay was for people just starting out in the service at that time. A private E-2, which is what I was made a whopping $72.00 a month. Minimum wage in civilian life was $1.60 per hour or $256.00 based on a 28-day month. The $72.00 a month is what most enlisted people made for the first 8 months to a year in the Army. Fortunately, thanks to President Nixon and the Army a bill was passed that changed the pay scales in late 1972 and then a private E-2 made $138.30. Close to a 100% increase but still about half of what the lowest paying jobs in civilian life made at that time.

Basic training was one of the most miserable yet rewarding eight weeks of my life. I had never been in such a structured environment like this before in my life, even my training at Marmion had not prepared me for all of what we would encounter in basic training. Later in life I would attend some of my son's basic training and it was much easier. Of course, that could have been because it was the Air Force. We were up at 0600 then out to do Physical Training (PT). Once we completed PT we had to run to the mess hall. We had thirty minutes for breakfast. Once that was over it was military training all day. This could be ten-mile marches, obstacle courses, and other fun things. Each day the workload got harder as they built up our stamina. We went through a gas chamber and were told to take off our masks. Then tear gas was released. You had to stay in the chamber until everyone had their mask off and we had to sing Yankee Doodle Dandy! It was not a fun experience. We were issued rifles and told to memorize the serial numbers. We then learned to take them apart and clean them blindfolded. I think I could still take an M-16 apart and clean it quickly, but probably not blindfolded anymore.

Our next adventure came on the grenade range. This was an interesting place. We all got to throw two live grenades at targets about twenty meters away. We were throwing from within a special trench that had a hole in the bottom that looked like a drain with no cover. This was in case someone dropped their grenade after they had pulled the pin. The instructor could kick the live grenade down the hole so that when it exploded no one got hurt. I mentioned one guy from our platoon that got recycled. He dropped his grenade and the Sergeant in charge had to kick it into the hole. He then yelled "fire in the hole," and we all hit the ground. Now you know why he got recycled. Then there was more obstacle course training, and finally the confidence course. On the way to the confidence course the weather was very cold, and it had not rained for a couple of days. I saw something I had never seen before. The puddles in the road were covered in dust. You thought you were marching along on a flat surface and then suddenly you were in a six-inch-deep hole full of water. After hitting a few of these the sergeant let us swerve around them rather than go straight through them. I guess he wanted to be nice to us because he knew what was coming up next. On the confidence course where we were exposed to live fire rounds. We had to crawl about seventy-five yards under barb wire that was less than sixteen inches off the ground. M-60 machine guns were firing live rounds over our heads and additionally, explosives were being detonated around us. We were mostly faced down as we were crawling but when one of the explosives went off, I had to turn over. The concussion had knocked my helmet off, so I had to retrieve it without going above the wire. I wondered after I got my helmet back, if I held it above the wire would the bullets hit it? I only thought about it and did not actually do it. We were told that some trainees had been hit by bullets on the confidence course, but I am not sure if that really happened or if that was something they told us to keep us on our toes. All I do know is that when we completed basic training, I was proud of what I had become and glad that I had made the decision to join the Army. Enlisting in the Army in 1970 was not a popular choice. There were protest all over the country about the Vietnam War. There were also draft dodgers who fled the country to Canada to avoid being drafted, and students who went to college just to avoid getting drafted because of student deferments. Fortunately, there were enough people who felt servicing their country was the right thing to do. I was proud to serve my country.

After basics it was off to Fort Lee Virginia to attend 76P20 training, also known as Stock Control and Accounting. This was an eight-week training class. I really enjoyed this training and did very well at it. The only downside was that during this class everyone in the class was POR'ed (Processed for Overseas Replacement), which meant it was highly likely that you were going to Vietnam. The POR training consisted of two days of going through basic jungle training so that you knew what to look for in various boobie traps that were being used by the enemy at the time. I am sure we did not see every kind of trap that existed, but we saw enough to not want to see them live. As it turned out the lower half of the 76P20 class were sent to Vietnam, and those who finished in the upper half of the class were sent to various other supply schools. The upper half of the class also received promotions for their achievement. In most classes this was a promotion to the rank of Private E-2, In my case since I was already an E-2, I was promoted to E-3, Private First Class. Since I finished in the upper quarter of the class, and was the only one promoted to PFC, I got first choice for my next school. I selected 76R20 training, also known as Missile Repair Parts Specialist. This sounded like the most interesting school to attend. All the quartermaster courses were taught in Fort Lee, Virginia at that time. This was a six-week course and since we had no missile bases in Vietnam, most of us who attended that class were going to be sent to Europe, Korea, or bases in the United States. I finished this class in the top 10% and was promoted again. This time I was promoted to E-4 Specialist Four. I was now at the rank of Specialist Four in less than eight months, instead of eighteen months or up to two years that it normally takes to attain that rank. All of this was jumpstarted by a decision I made when I was twelve years old to go to a Marmion Military Academy.

While attending the two courses at Fort Lee, we did get to go into town on weekends and we could earn a three-day pass for good behavior. The town was a small town called Petersburg. It was about twenty-seven miles from Richmond, Virginia and only a couple of miles outside of the base. It was an interesting place. Half of the townspeople loved us because soldiers spent money in town, and half the townspeople disliked us because they considered us a bad element. I am sure a few soldiers did cause issues in town, but I did not see anything that could have been considered a genuine problem. Mostly we visited a few bars and then went to the liquor store to pick up some Boone Farm Wine. This was the beverage of choice because it was extremely cheap, and all the beer on base was what they called three-two beers. It was half the alcohol content of regular beer, so you really had to drink a lot to feel it. There really was no place else to go in the area that was of interest to a bunch of teenagers unless you had a three-day pass. We figured out how to get a three-day pass within a couple of weeks after arriving in Fort Lee. These could be earned by giving blood late Thursday afternoon after class. If you gave blood on Thursday, you got a pass that started Friday morning through Sunday at midnight. When this happened a couple of us hitchhiked to one of the other guy's houses in other states. I donated blood three times in the fourteen weeks I was at Fort Lee. This meant three adventures to unknown places. We always traveled in pairs as we hitchhiked just to be safe. My first trip was to Illinois to come back to my house. It was uneventful, so I did not do another trip to Illinois, plus it was a long trip for hitchhiking. The second was to Mount Holly in New Jersey. This one was interesting because there were two of us, and we got picked up by a couple of female college students. They started talking about the war in Vietnam and asked us how we could stand to be part of the military. We explained our view of the whole thing and they offered to drive us to Canada, so that we could desert. We both looked at each other and laughed. The rest of the ride to Mt. Holly was quiet. The trip back from Mount Holly would prove to be more interesting. We left early Sunday evening just like we always did on passes. We assumed that we would easily get a ride all the way back to Virginia. It did not turn out that way. We got as far as Maryland and figured out that we would not be able to get back to Fort Lee in time. We would have been late and that would have been considered Absent Without Leave (AWOL). We had been told in training that if you were on a pass and could not get to your own base that you should check into the nearest Army base. The nearest base to us at the time was Fort Meade in Maryland. We checked in with Military Police at that base and they just looked at us, shook their heads and told us to wait in the lobby. We had no idea what was going to happen. As it turned out, by turning ourselves in at the nearest Army post we were considered AWOL insufficient. In the Army this meant that we did not have the necessary funds to complete the required travel to our home base. In civilian speaking it would mean we were irresponsible and stupid. In this case I preferred the Army version of our condition. We spent two days at Fort Meade, and our job was to paint rocks white. I am not sure why, but the Army loves to paint rocks white and line them up along unpaved streets. The third time was very uneventful. We hitchhiked to Massillon, Ohio where my traveling companion Sam Gitto had lived before joining the Army. Sam was a football player in high school and immensely proud to have been a Massillon Tiger. Apparently, they were very well known at the time. Sam and I attended the same 76R20 course. This time we started out early enough on Sunday to make sure we would be back before our passes expired. Looking back at those hitchhiking trips now, I think this may have been some of the dumbest decisions I made in my life. We were in uniform, and the war was not popular in a lot of places. We could have been picked up by some radical group who wanted to punish soldiers or worse. I cannot imagine anyone hitchhiking around half the country now and thinking they were perfectly safe. I am confident that God was watching over us at the time.

C-130 Hercules

Chapter 9
Next Stop, not Vietnam

Upon graduation from 76R20 School (Missile Repair Parts Specialist), I received orders to go to Germany. My first assignment was to go to the Giessen Army Depot, and work in my MOS (Military Occupational Specialty) of Stock Control and Accounting. It was to be a two plus year assignment I thought I would be there for my entire Army career. I had never flown on a military transport flight before, so I did not know what to expect. I just grabbed my duffle bag and got in line to get on the C-130 Hercules transport (above). Once I got on the plane the fun began. I gave my duffle bag to one of the crew and he threw it behind a cargo net with about thirty other duffle bags. I then looked over the rest of the plane. It did not look anything like a normal civilian jet. All the seats faced the back of the plane. There were no windows, I guess that really did not matter, since they normally only carried cargo. The good news is that I knew they would not lose my luggage, because I could see it the entire flight. The seats looked like that had been procured out of Army jeeps and they did not adjust or recline. There was no flight attendance, no movie, and no meal service. I wondered what else might be missing. I found out about halfway through the fourteen-hour flight what else was missing. There were no actual restrooms! There was a curtain that you went behind that had bench with a hole in it. Thankfully, this was a prop plane, so it was extremely loud on the flight, and no one could hear you taking care of your business behind the curtain. At some point, one of the crew handed us a box of K-ration so we had something to eat. The next part of the adventure occurred when the pilot learned that our flight was being diverted to the Azore Islands off the coast of Portugal, instead of the intended refueling stop. We learned that this change of course was due to fact that the President of the United States was going to land in Rhein-Main Air Force Base in Frankfurt around the same time that we were supposed to land. It turns out that the Azore Islands off the coast of Portugal are beautiful. In fact, when we landed there, I thought we had landed in Hawaii by mistake. We stayed in the Azores for about eight hours, so we got to look around and meet the natives before we continued our trip to Rhein-Main AFB in Frankfurt, Germany. This trip and its diversion were not something I planned, but I am glad it happened. It made me appreciate commercial airlines and took me to a place that I would never have dreamed of going to before that flight.

However, when I got to Germany things changed. I received new orders, because there were no openings in the Army Depot at Giessen in my field at that time. I was instead sent to Battery A, 6/517th Artillery Battery, which was a Hawk Missile Battery. I was not sure what they had planned for me, but I was sure I was not going to like it. Additionally, when I arrived at the 517th and they saw that I was a Specialist 4, and that I had the word "missile" in my training, so they decided to put me in charge of a Hawk missile battery. Not only that but they made me the missile crew chief! So, with no training on the Hawk missile, I was to supervise a crew of three men. Our job was the maintenance of this "towed" missile launcher, and to be prepared to fire the missiles if the need arose. On the surface, it seemed to be something that would be relatively easy if you had been trained on hawk missiles. To make sure that our missiles were ready we had to test these missiles to simulate an actual attack. This consisted of taking a panel off the warhead on the top left side of the missile and attaching a little black box that would override the actual firing of the missile and simulate the missile firing with a series of lights. The first time I had to arm the missiles for test firing was a little scary. If I did not connect the override panel correctly the missiles could fire and take out one of the actual planes we used as targets. Fortunately, I did not create any international incidents by shooting down any planes by accident. No telling how things would have turned out if I had made such a fatal mistake. I do not even want to think about it.

I did this job for a few months. We worked shifts that were called "manning," they consisted of twenty-four hours on and twenty-four hours off. We also had to pull guard duty at our remote location, and it was starting to get cold in Germany. We also did field exercises on an alert basis. We did not know when they were going to occur. It could be at any time, and we would pack our field gear and head out to some remote woodland in the middle of nowhere. This was when I started looking for a better opportunity within the battery. It turned out that the Colonel, who oversaw the Battery was looking for a new driver. He wanted someone who was at least a Specialist 4 for the job with a clean driving record. I had not had any opportunity to drive in the military at that point, so my military driving record was clean. I volunteered for the job. This was my first good decision while in the Artillery. I had to take a jeep driving test that was easy to pass. It consisted of a two-hour movie on the proper handling of a light military utility vehicle, and then a road test on said vehicle. I still had to go out on the various field exercises, but now I did not have to sleep in a two-man tent in below freezing weather. It turns out the Colonel had a two and half ton covered truck that had three cots in it. One for him, one for his aide, and one for his designated driver. I did not know how long the Colonel would be with the battalion, so my future was unsure, but it was good for the short term. If we were not in the field all I had to do was to maintain the Colonel's jeep instead of maintaining missiles.

Hawk Missile Battery (towed)

Many of the people who end up in combat arms units like the infantry, armored, or artillery are there because they were drafted, and really did not want to be in the Army or did not have skills that the Army could use elsewhere. Others were just Gung Ho and had very unusual ways of entertaining themselves. We lived in huge stone and brick buildings that had been used in World War II by the Germans. Based on how well they were made, I think the Germans planned on usings them for a long time. I remember watching some of the artillery people jumping out the second story window of the barracks and seeing who could make the best landing as they yelled "Airborne." The only equipment they used for this entertainment was a lot of beer.

After eight months, I decided that I did not want to be in the artillery. I wanted to work in the MOS that I had been trained in. I just did not fit in with the men who had selected or been drafted into the artillery or their approach to entertainment. I was sure that, based on my size, that one of these giants would throw me out the window to see if I could fly at some point. To change to another assignment, the army had a program in which you could restart your enlistment. It was called taking a short tour. This was basically reenlisting, but you only had eight months added to your enlistment. It was only available if you had been in the service for less than one year. If you chose to participate in this program, it would allow you to select any location in the same theater of action provided they had an opening in your field. In this case it meant I could select anywhere in Europe. I chose to go to Italy, so that I could work in my actual MOS that I had been trained for back in Fort Lee, Virginia. No telling what would have happened if I had stayed in Germany, but this turned out to be my second good decision while in the Artillery. So, I said Auf Weiders Ehen to Germany.

Caserne Ederle-Vicenza, Italy

Chapter 10
Welcome to Italy

My arrival in Italy was interesting. Since I was traveling by myself, I was given a set orders and a train ticket to Vicenza, Italy. My orders were to report to Southern European Task Force (SETAF) headquarters at Caserne Ederle in Vicenza, Italy for my new assignment. The train trip itself was uneventful, but the scenery was amazing. We traveled through parts of the Alps and then through the Dolomites as we entered Italy. European trains are much different than trains in the United States. Train cars look like something from an old movie. Sort of a poor man's version of the Orient Express. My ticket was not for first class seating, but it was still nice. Except there was no dining car, so trying to get something to eat was a challenge. The train would make several short stops at little towns along the way. I started watching the locals on the train to see how they got food since the stops were not long enough to find a restaurant. The trick was to catch one of the street vendors, who were hawking their wares to the passengers hanging out of the windows of the train when it made one of these whistle-stops.

I gave one of the vendors three US dollars. I figured that they would accept US currency and that seemed like the right amount for a sandwich. I had no idea what the exchange rate was at time, but he gave me some kind of sandwich. Later I learned that the sandwich was called a panini. I had no idea what kind of meat was on it, but I was very hungry, so I'd try anything. Later I was told it was probably horsemeat! I never found out for sure what it was and never saw that type of meat again.

Once I arrived in Vicenza, I started getting lots of questions from the locals. At first, I was not sure why until I started to look around and noticed that most of the people looked like me. I am half Italian and half Belgium but look more Italian, so I assume they thought that I would speak Italian. Unfortunately, I did not speak any Italian at the time. So, I would tell the people in English that I did not speak Italian. They would then walk away with a puzzled look on their faces as to why I could not help them. Hopefully, they would find someone else who could assist them and did not think that I was just an ugly American.

I had heard a lot about Italian coffee from my grandfather and my mother, so I decided to have some. I went into a trattoria and order my first Italian coffee. I ordered an espresso, which I thought would be like our coffee at home and was shocked when it came in a tiny little cup! I figured I must have ordered a small coffee, so I drank it. I was shocked at how strong it was and the caffeine level. I left the trattoria so wired that I thought I could have run to the base. Once I arrived at the base via taxi, I was told to report to the headquarters building of the 5th Battalion, 30th Field Artillery. They intern told me that I was going to an Ordinance platoon that was at some place called the BLSA (Basic Load Storage Area). I had no idea what this was, but I soon found out that it was a remote location away from the base. I was to work with a small detachment of ten men. Our job was to make sure that the twelve Pershing Missiles with warheads were always ready if needed. My job was to keep all the necessary parts on hand to make sure we could update any software or replace the parts that were needed. The Pershing missiles were huge. The warheads alone were as big as the Hawk missiles I had worked on in Germany. I learned shortly after arrival that the warheads were armed, and I then understood why each one was in a separate underground bunker. I was told that the warheads were nuclear, but I never found out for sure. Ironically, the storage area was directly below the Commanding General's house. I guess if there was an accident, the General wanted to know what happened firsthand! Personally, I thought it was an unwise decision on his part, but I am sure that the rent on the villa was inexpensive. After all, with all the beautiful views available in the area, why would you pick want to stay at a place where all you saw was barb wire and bombs.

Pershing Warheads

Basic Load Storage Area

Most of my time in Italy was very routine. We drove about twenty miles to and from the remote site every day and if we were not maintaining the missiles, we would be cleaning our vehicles or guarding the missiles. At night, we go to the base theater and see a movie or go downtown Vicenza and go to one of the local bars. While in Italy, I was promoted to Specialist Five (E-5) on April 1, 1972. I was on the fast track for promotions because of the decision I made when I was twelve years old. I was told that I had made Specialist 5 in less time than anyone in the command. I had made it in less than eighteen months from the day I started in the Army. Since I was thinking about staying in, I started taking additional college courses. I knew that would help me move up through the ranks if I decided to stay in the service. I knew that the next promotion would require a lot more education and training. Promotion to the rank of E-6 was centralized so you were competing against every other E-5 in the same skill specialty throughout the Army.

All that changed on September 5, 1972, when eight Palestinian terrorists, representing the militant group "Black September," broke into the Olympic Village, killing two members of the Israeli team and taking nine hostages—ironically, all this occurred only twenty kilometers from the site of one of the concentration camps from World War II. I was very thankful that I was no longer stationed in Germany at the time.

Terrorist at the Munich Olympics 1972

All the U.S., bases in Europe were put on high alert. No one knew if this was an isolated incident or if there might be other attacks. Several checkpoints were set up throughout Germany, and Italy. Since our base housed warheads, we were assigned bomb details inspecting all incoming vehicles to the main base at Caserne Ederle. Back then this consisted of giving us mirrors so we could look under the vehicles and search the interiors and trunks for explosive devices. We heard about a case of a bomb going off at one of the other checkpoints, but it did result in any injuries. Again, I was fortunate that it was not my checkpoint.

Overall, my tour of duty in Italy was great. It was so good that I decided I would make the army a career. I set up a meeting with the re-enlistment sergeant and took some more aptitude test for re-enlistment to determine what I was most qualified to be in services. The test showed that there were two choices that stood out for me based on the results of the test and the needs of the Army. One was to be an Office Equipment Repairmen (91J20), and the other was to Electronic Test Equipment Repairman (35B20). I decided that the second option had more future potential, so I reenlisted for 3 more years. The Army gave me a re-enlistment bonus based on my current job in Missile Repair Parts. The bonus was $4,000 and no taxes! I thought it was funny that they would give a bonus based on my current training to have me go to a different Military Operations Specialty (MOS). I was to go to signal school in Fort Gordon, Georgia. The initial training course for the 35B20 course was to be for twenty-six weeks. I then bid arrivederci to Vicenza, Italy in September of 1972. The Army paid all my expenses for the move because I was a Specialist 5 (E-5). This was one of the best choices I had made while I was in the Army. Little did I know the adventures that it would lead to over the rest of my military service.

Chapter 11
Georgia on My Mind

ort Gordon was an interesting place. All Signal School training was conducted at Fort Gordon at the time. The fort was located outside the town of Augusta, Georgia. This was the first time I had even been stationed in the south. This was in the seventies, and there were still bars that were divided in half between Black people and white people. These bars had one bartender and one bar but a barrier in the middle separating the two colors. I also saw places where there were two drinking fountains next to each other, one saying for whites only. Since my first three years in the army were either in school or overseas this was really my first glimpse of discrimination. I did not see the point. I had worked with several Black soldiers up to this point and they seemed to be the same as I was so I just could not see why anyone would go to all the trouble of trying to keep things separated. I felt like I had gone back in time. Once I reported for my duty assignment, I found myself in a unique position as a student. I was a Specialist Five with a couple of years in service and almost all the students in my platoon were either private (E-2) just coming out of basic training or Specialist Four (E-4) in their second classes. I outranked all my fellow students in the 35B class and the other students in my platoon who were enrolled in other classes at the same location. Based on my rank, I was made the platoon leader, in charge of all the students, to make sure everyone got to class on time and behaved properly. I reported directly to Sergeant First Class (E-7) Rivera, who was part of the company cadre for battalion.

I am not sure if it was because of my rank or because I did well in class, but the Army decided that I should go to a second electronics school. This was Electronic Test Equipment Maintenance (35B30). I would end up staying at Fort Gordon for another 16 weeks. I finally left Fort Gordon in September of 1973, anxious to get started in my new skill specialty. Unfortunately, the Army could not figure out what to do with me at that time, so I was temporarily sent to Fort McClellan, Alabama.

When I got to Fort McClellan, they assigned me to the Directorate of Industrial Operations as a Communications and Electronics Specialist. My job was to coordinate activity on the various firing ranges and make sure that all the electronic equipment was working. These firing ranges were primary for tanks and artillery units accompanied by ground troops. They were using live artillery rounds and small arms ammunition when on these ranges. The units on the ranges were mostly National Guard and Army Reserve. The goal was to keep them away from each other to insure no one was injured or killed in training. I reported directly to Captain Cobb. He was a West Point graduate and highly respected in the Army community. I did this from October of 1973 to July of 1974. I was recommended for my first Army Commendation Medal, but it was downgraded to a Certificate of Achievement. The Certificate of Achievement stated basically that I had profound innovative abilities and applied creative solutions to areas of need. I did not think I deserved the Army Commendation Medal for what I had done at Fort McClellan, so I am glad that it got downgraded. Captain Cobb, who recommended me for the medal, told me why he had recommended me for the ARCOM. He said he knew the Army would downgrade the recommendation, so he went one level higher than what he wanted me to get. It was a smart decision on his part. I really enjoyed my time at Fort McClellan because I oversaw so many things that could impact many soldiers. During my time at Fort McClellan there were zero accidents on any of the firing ranges that we were responsible for, and considering the wide variety of units using the ranges this was quite an accomplishment.

Chapter 12
That's Classified

Then in early July, I finally got orders that would allow me to work as an electronics equipment specialist. The orders showed I was being assigned to USASAFSA in Germany. My first reaction was to try and figure out what this acronym stood for. I tried to ask several people, but no one seemed to know what the nature of the assignment was, just that it was in Germany. I knew something was up because Government agents had visited my parents as part of the security background check on me. I hoped that my mother had not alienated any of the agents. I had a vision of her giving them a piece of her mind and their leaving shaking their heads. Finally, I was contacted directly by the Agency and told that I was to report to the United States Army Security Agency Field Station Augsburg in Germany. I had been selected to be a part of what was considered the top 10% of the Army. This was one of the twists that happened in your life that you had no idea it was going to happen, but you are glad that it did.

Field Station Antenna (elephant cage)

Old system with RM-15 scopes

When I left the United States for Germany, I landed at Munich International Airport. Munich is about thirty miles from Augsburg, and I was able to take a shuttle bus to the base at Gablingen Kaserne. I reported into the Supply & Maintenance (S & M) Company of the Augsburg Field Station. I was told that starting the next day, I would report to the Field Station which was located just north of the base. Since Field Station ran twenty-four hours a day there was shuttle service every hour between the Kaserne and the Field Station. Our overall mission was to electronically monitor communications from the Soviet Union, East Germany, and northern Africa. This was done via a massive antenna (Above), which we affectionately call the elephant cage. I was assigned to a group called Test Maintenance Diagnostic Equipment or TMDE for short. We were a part of the Systems Engineering Division (SED). Our team had the highest security clearances at the site in Augsburg because we needed access to all areas of the site. We also got to dress differently than all the other soldiers who were in normal Army uniforms. It was important that for security reasons we could be easily identified by the people operating the workstations. We wore coveralls that displayed the SED logo (below). Additionally, different ranks had special colors so that the operators in the various areas could easily find out who was in charge. Officers wore yellow coveralls, Non-Commissioned E-6 and above wore orange coveralls, and E-5s and below wore green coveralls. This system made it easier for us to move around the site because we could be easily identified as the technicians who would make all that all the equipment work.

TMDE's job specifically was the testing, repair, and calibration of any equipment that was used by the code breakers, communications people, and linguists in support of their radio equipment. Most of the items we repaired were devices that we had seen in school, however, due to the specialized nature of ASA, we often ended up repairing something that we had never seen before. We even fixed equipment on occasions that we did not know existed! One of the most unusual items that I was tasked to repair was something called a Time Domain Reflectometer (TDR). My first task was to figure out how it worked and what it was used for at the field station. As it turned out it was an extremely important unit, and there were only two of them in the entire field station. Since one of them was sitting on my bench in front of me, I knew that I needed to make sure I got this one fixed right and I had nothing to reference since the other one was currently out being used on the large circular antenna system, we called the elephant cage. It turns out that this device would find weak spots or breaks in the cable that was used throughout the entire antenna. The antenna was circular and as big as two football fields in diameter, so I had to make a scaled down version of the system to evaluate and repair the TDR. I started looking around our shop and saw a couple of 100 ft spools of coaxial cable. I decided that if I put a connector on one end of each of them, I could do some simulation of the testing needed to ensure the TDR was operating correctly. I started with one completely intact spool to use it as reference of what I should get on an unbroken cable. Now that I have a reference, I was able to apply marks on the cable at different points on the other spool. One imitating a complete break in the case, one imitating a break in the shielding around the cable and one cut through the center cable, but still connected to the rest of the spool. My experiment worked and I was able to tell the exact weak points of all three flaws I had created and their distance from the connector. The team that used the TDR was incredibly happy to get their back up unit back knowing that it now worked accurately. My boss was not happy that I wrecked a 100-foot spool of coaxial cable, but when I told him that we now had a standard that we could use for future repairs if we had any other issues with the TDRs. My boss was OK with what I had done even though it was not regulation. I did not get any credit from the Army for this new standard that I had developed, but since there were only two of these units per field station, it probably would not have saved the Army much money anyway. That was not the case with my next modification.

Since the field station ran continuously 24 hours a day, it was critical that downtime on all equipment was minimized. I noticed over a couple of months that we had overheating problems with one type of oscilloscope that was mounted in the racks used to monitor communications from the Soviet Union and East Germany. I removed one of the scopes and put it in a loaner scope so that I could try and recreate the problem. All these scopes had several tubes in them. When the RM-15 oscilloscope was out of the rack it worked fine, but when it was in the rack it would overheat. All the racks had fans to dissipate heat already, so I knew I needed to devise something additional that could address the overheating issue with the one tube that was causing the problem. I was determined to permanently cure this problem. I was tired of getting calls to repair the same item. I designed a heat sync that went around the offending tube to help dissipate heat and put it back in the rack. The fix worked and the RM-15 oscilloscope no longer overheated. I submitted my design for the modification of the RM-15 oscilloscopes used in the racks (above). The army gave me an award citation for the modification, and it was installed at all ASA sites worldwide. This also came with a check for about $1,500. The money was based on 1% of what the army felt was saved by the reduction of failures to the RM-15's. My decision to solve this issue may not have had an impact on world peace, but I know it kept a lot of soldiers, whose job it was to monitor those scopes happy. Since the overheating problem has been resolved.

In late 1975, I was selected for a special assignment within ASA. I believe I was selected because of having a background in both supply and firsthand equipment repair experience. I may have been the only one in Germany who had the right combination of skills that the Army wanted for this part of the project. The army was completely replacing the current system used at the Field Station in Augsburg at the time. The new secret project was code named La Faire Vite (Pictured below). My job was to identify all the parts that could potentially break down once the system was operational and develop stockage levels so that the key items were readily available if needed. I stayed on the project until I ETS (End Term of Service) in September 1977. I was awarded the Army Commendation Medal for my performance with the Army Security Agency from August 1974 through September 1977. It reads as follows:

"Throughout his assignment, he consistently displayed outstanding qualities of ingenuity, integrity, and professional competence. The energetic application of his extensive knowledge and experience, coupled with his reliability for completing projects of significant importance, contributed in large measure to the successful accomplishment of this Command's highly complex mission. His selfless devotion to the military service reflects great credit upon himself, his organization, and the United States Army."

Just prior to my end of service the Army tried to get me to reenlist. They wanted me to be a recruiter because of how quickly I had risen through the ranks, and that I had received my Bachelor of Science degree while I was in the Army. I graduated Cum Laude from the University of Maryland after about five years of classes at night. I told them that if they would get me an assignment as a recruiter in Chicago I would consider staying for another three years. They came back and told me that they could get me an assignment as a recruiter in Milwaukee. I thought about it but felt that the Army was not something I wanted long term anymore. If I had chosen to stay, my future would have been completely different, and I would not have met my future wife. I am confident that my decision to resign after seven years was the right decision. I do not think I could ever have anticipated the path that led me through all the twists and turns of my army career. Little did I know what the future had in store for me in civilian life.

SED Logo for My team

La Faire Vite

Chapter 13
The Wander Years

Once I left the service I returned to St. Charles, Illinois, and started looking for a job. I had sent out about fifteen or twenty resumes in my last month in the Army. Most of them were sent to larger electronic firms. I thought with my security clearance and background in electronics I would get someone to make me an offer. No acceptable offers came from that group. I also sent out my resume to local companies for management positions in the Fox Valley area where I planned on living. I was truly fortunate and found a job in less than two weeks. I went to work for a company called Marketing Central. Marketing Central was a distribution center for the National Industrial Brass Company (NIBCO). Marketing Central sold all types of plumbing and fire prevention parts to various plumbing wholesalers and some larger end users. We also distributed fire prevention products. What we distributed was more interesting than I thought it would be when I started. I learned a lot about the various things used for installing plumbing and the correct applications of these items. I got hired by the general manager of Marketing Central, his name was Dwight Cochran. Dwight told me that he hired me because of my military background. He felt that I would have strong organizational skills and make an excellent office manager. Little did I know that this job would completely alter my future direction and impact both my working and personal life for the next 50 years. The decision to take the job at Marketing Central had been the right choice. Especially since it was the only job offer that I got at the time.

At Marketing Central I ran an office that included eight people. Three of the people managed parts inventories and the other five people had administrative jobs like processing orders, billing, and answering phones. The five administrative people were all women. One of the administrative people was a young lady who prepared most of the sales orders. At the time this involved a lot of typing customer orders, and she was an amazingly fast typist. She seemed shy at first but opened the more we worked together. I took all the office staff out to lunch occasionally and found that I was very attracted to this one young lady. Her name was Cindy. After a while we started dating. We were both divorced at the time. She inspired me to do things I had not done in my previous life. I started authoring poems for her and even ended up writing our wedding vows. Little did I know that meeting her and falling in love with her would forever change our future. After dating for a while we got engaged and started planning a date to get married. We selected March 22nd because we wanted a spring wedding to signify our new beginning together. So, on the 22nd of March 1980, we were married in the Methodist Church in St. Charles. We could not afford an expensive wedding since we were paying for the wedding ourselves, but we wanted a church wedding and a nice reception. We both maxxed out our credit cards for the wedding and our Florida honeymoon. Over the next few years our working lives would be a series of overlapping companies beginning with Marketing Central. None of the overlaps were planned, they just happened. You might call it fate. I have no doubt that marrying Cindy was the smartest decision that I ever would make in my life. Without her, I would have become a completely different person, and not for the better! God only knows what I would be without her. Now, over forty-four years later she is still the one.

The sales department at Marketing Central always looked like they were having fun and really enjoyed selling. It seemed to be a lot more exciting than being an office manager. I decided that I should find a job in sales. I saw an ad in the local newspaper for sales manager for a plumbing and electrical department at a company called St. Charles Wholesale. This company was an independent home center. I interviewed for the job and got offered the sales manager position and I left Marketing Central. St. Charles Wholesale was one of several companies owned and operated by the Siegle family. My job at St. Charles Wholesale was as the manager of the plumbing and electrical departments. It was a wonderful job! I reported directly to the store manager. His name was Don Brodie. Don gave me a lot of freedom to run my department. He also let me dabble in other departments in the store. I eventually learned about everything you would buy at a home center except the lumber department. Don taught me one thing that I have continued to use in my thinking for the rest of my working life.

Don said, "Your first loss is your best loss."

In this case he was talking about items that did not sell and lowering the prices. I took it as looking at a situation, decide on what to do, and do not dwell on it.

On a normal day, confused customers would come in and tell me about the problem they were having with something in their homes, and I would help them find creative solutions to solve the problems. Sometimes it was as easy as knowing about that one part they did not know about. At other times I would have to be creative and build a fix for their problem. Either way it was a lot of fun. This job was key to my learning how to think creatively. This ability would serve me well for the rest of my life.

As it so happened the Siegle's had a job opening for a secretary to the president in their Elgin Lumber location. I thought Cindy would be a natural for the job. She interviewed and went to work for Harold and Harry Siegle at Elgin Lumber. This became our second time working for the same company and would lead us down the path to another industry together. Cindy left Elgin Lumber in 1980. She was tired of the long drive to work in Elgin. She wanted to work somewhere closer to St. Charles. She ended up taking a position at a company called Gordon Flesch Company (GFC). They were a company that distributed copiers to business. They were an old company that started in the 1950's and they are still in business today. Their headquarters was in Madison Wisconsin when she worked at GFC. Her job involved working on service contracts to make sure customers were billed for the correct meter counts on the machines that were under service contracts. She ended up doing a little bit of everything at GFC. The general manager at the St. Charles location for GFC was an interesting fellow named Bob Bangert. He was one of the most likable people I have met in my life. He had the ability to get everyone to like him. He was loud and funny and could have easily been Santa Claus in his previous life. As fortune would have it the office of GFC was only about a block away from St. Charles Wholesale, so Bob would often come in to buy things that they needed at his office. I would often help him pick out the right things for something he was trying to fix at the office.

Chapter 14

So, You Want to Sell Copiers

Since Bob was so outgoing, he would always strike up a conversation with me and anyone else who would listen at St. Charles Wholesale. Bob's location for Gordon Flesch was doing well, and he was looking to expand the number of salespeople that they employed. The copier business was a very tough job and had a high turnover of sales personnel. Cindy thought that I might want to discuss a possible job with Bob. At first, Bob was not interested in me because I did not have any outside sales experience. He tried to talk me out of selling copiers. He told me that if I did take a job with GFC, and it turned out I could not sell copiers he would fire me. Well, that was all I needed to really pursue the job. Once someone tells me that I cannot do something I have to try and do it. This became my third job in three years. I hoped my wandering was over and that my decision to leave the security of my managers job at St. Charles Wholesale and take a chance on an outside sales job was the right decision. Little did I know that the stars had aligned for the copier industry just three years earlier.

Prior to 1976 Xerox controlled the copier machine industry. They had 94% of the copier market and protected their technology with over 2,000 patents. The process to make plain paper copies was invented in 1938 by a man named Chester Carlson. He originally called the process electrophotography. He later changed the name to Xerography, from the Greek language meaning "dry writing." It took him over ten years to find a company that would develop his process for commercial use. He finally found a company called the Haloid Company, located in Rochester, New York, to collaborate with him on his process. It took several years for the Haloid Company to produce their first commercial copier. They had changed their name to Xerox, and in 1959 they introduced the first commercial dry powder copier called Xerox 914 (below). I will come up against this product later, but that is another story. In my days with Gordon Flesch, I had the honor to replace a 914 copier in 1982. I am not sure when it was installed originally but it was still running at the time and had to be at least twenty years old. For the next seventeen years Xerox had exclusive rights to this process. However, in 1976 the government stepped in and ruled that Xerox's control of this process was in violation of the anti-trust act. Xerox was required to give several Japanese companies access to Xerox's technology. This opened the floodgates for companies like Canon, Sharp, Ricoh, and Toshiba to start selling their "Xerographic" technology copiers in the US. I was lucky enough to be in the right place at the right time to be on the upswing of this now competitive market.

Xerox 914

NP400F

I went to work for Gordon Flesch Company in 1980 as a salesperson. Being in outside sales back then was pretty much like being thrown to the wolves as to what you had to learn and do to sell. To work for Gordon Flesch, you had to buy a full-size van to carry three copy machines, and you were paid a draw against commissions. No salary, no expense account, just a draw against commissions. There were five salespeople at the time that I was hired at Gordon Flesch. And most of them were focused on making sales for themselves. They saw little benefit to helping some new guy who had never been an outside salesperson before.

On my first day, Bob assigned me a sales territory and told me to go out and start cold calling businesses in my territory. Little did I know that since the market had become so competitive so quickly that customers were not incredibly open to people calling on them without an appointment. In my territory, I could only sell the Canon brand of copiers for Gordon Flesch. The Canon brand was a new line for them. I was the first salesperson that Bob Bangert hired who would have a territory that directly competed with someone else from Gordon Flesch in the same territory. Bob Bangert decided that if he had two salespeople with different product lines, we would have better coverage and sell more products. I competed directly with a salesperson with ten years of experience selling copiers. His name was Bob Hansen, and he sold Savin copiers, which Gordon Flesch had been selling since they opened their office some twelve years earlier. Bob Hanson looked at me as an interloper in his territory.

So, I was on my own, either learning to sell or get fired. I started knocking on doors of businesses and asking them about what they had for their copiers. I would then tell them that I had a better solution for them and would be glad to show them my product. Since we had our copiers with us and could show the customer right away, we seemed to have an advantage over the competition. I think that fact appealed to the potential customer. You still had to knock on a lot of doors to find someone who would let you show them the product. I believe I called on over two hundred companies in my first month. I did demonstrations on copiers for ten companies and sold three copiers in my first month. I can still remember the first three sales I made. One was a small doctor's office in West Chicago, who bought a new NP-120 copier. The second was a print shop in Wheaton, who bought a rental NP-400F (above). It was our largest copier. It had to be hilarious to see a 140-pound soaking wet little salesperson pushing around a 400-pound copier on a cart that looked like a hospital gurney walking down the street. The third sale may have been the most satisfying. It was a used NP-200 that I sold to Chimney Sweep company in Barrington. It was a lead that another salesperson at GFC gave me because he said I would never get approval for this company because they had poor credit. I looked at Mike Messmer, who gave me the lead and told him that I would not only sell them a copier, but that it would be paid for in cash. Mike agreed to the bet, which was for lunch, and I won the bet. Mike never took me to lunch.

After the first month I decided that to get better at this selling business, I needed to see how successful salespeople approached selling, so I asked two of my peers if I could ride with them for a day. The first was a Black gentleman named Clarence Baker. I picked him because he was the best dresser at the office, and he was a smooth talker. I learned a lot from Clarence, but the two most important things I learned from him were to dress for success and to always be polite when talking to potential customers. In those days, companies saw several door-to-door salespeople in a week, and quite often they got a little abrasive from all the salespeople calling on their offices.

The second salesperson I traveled with was a gentleman named George Powell. He was a large Black man, who at first glance was very intimidating. However, George was a gentle giant. He never swore and was always cheery and soft-spoken. From him, I learned the art of being patient with your potential customers. He had a way of making people feel receptive and wanted to listen to what he had to say.

I am confident that my decision to ask George and Clarence for help were keys to my becoming successful with Gorden Flesch. Success at Gordon Flesch was measured by sales. There were points awarded toward an annual trip based on attaining trip quota. I was a GFC for 10 years and won a trip every year. I sold just under 1,000 copiers and facsimile machines over my ten years at GFC.

Chapter 15
Close Calls

After the first few sales they all seem to run together, nothing noteworthy happened on the sales themselves. During my time at Gordon Flesch, I can recall two things that changed my perspective on life. The first occurred when Bob Bangert told me that he had a customer in Carol Stream who was delinquent on his bill, and that I needed to go out to see him and tell him that I needed to get a check from him for the overdue balance, or that I would have to remove our copier from his print shop. He did not take it well. He told me that he would pay when he could pay and that I should get out. I insisted that he pay us now, and he produced a pistol from his desk, and aimed it at me directly. He informed me that if I did not leave now, he would shoot me as an intruder. Discretion being the better part of valor, I promptly left the building. From this narrow escape, I learned to always know what you are walking into, and do not argue with a man with gun!

I scheduled a demonstration with Mr. Groves, who was the purchasing agent for this company in Carol Stream called Spraying Systems. He showed me the machine that they wanted to replace. It was a Xerox 914 in real life. I went out to my van and rolled out my brand-new Canon NP-400F, which weighs more than three hundred pounds. It was on a gurney, like what you would see in an ambulance and rolled it up to the warehouse door. The threshold was about four inches high, and the wheels needed to be lifted over the threshold front and then back. I asked Mr. Grove to lift the handle on the front of the cart for just a second so that I could come around and lift it over the threshold. Apparently, Mr. Groves did not hear what I said exactly, and he squeezed the level that unlocked the wheels on the cart. The cart went crashing straight down, but it did not hit the ground. It folded down quickly onto my leg, which was now trapped under the cart. I slowly pushed the top of the cart up so the wheels would lock in place and looked over the copier. I had to clean off some toner from the inside but proceeded to take the machine inside to do the demonstration. I asked Mr. Groves to assemble the people who needed to see the unit and get ready for my demo. Once the three people who needed to see the unit were present.

I said to Mr. Groves, "You saw how tough the Canon copier was earlier. Now if it makes perfect copies after what just happened would it be the right product for your company?"

He smiled and told me that if it still worked after what happened and it makes copies as good as you said then we will buy one to start with if the price is right. He said, "Remember I will eventually buy eight more if everything works out well."

And the rest was copier history. I had the honor of replacing the 648- pound Xerox 914 copier from their office. I am not sure how long they had this copier, but it had to be at least twenty years old, and it was still working. This copier was extremely large. When I took it in trade it had to be loaded into my van with a forklift and it filled up the van. I ended up selling this same company nine total Canon copiers over the years. I guess the copier cart collapsing on my leg was fate intervening on my behalf, I could not have planned such an event.

At Gordon Flesch Company, we also sold Savin copiers. When I first started the Savin units were sold by a separate sales team. Bob changed that after my first two years and made it an open competition where both sales teams being able to sell either product line. The Canon units were much better for copy quality, but the Savin copiers could make two sided copies without any issues since they did not heat up the paper. Two-sided copiers had not yet been invented. The way you made two sided copies was to reinsert the paper into the tray and turn over the original. Since the Savin copiers were liquid, you had to drain them before you took them out to the demonstration and reinstall the two supplies at the customer's location. The two supplies being toner and dispersant. The dispersant which was clear liquid could take tar off your car or light your grill. The toner was black and was in a self-sealing container that fit into a hole in the dispersant tray. I set up a demonstration to show one of the Savin products to an attorney in Aurora. He wanted a used copier because he wanted a good deal. We only sold Savin copiers used at the time. I should have known that this was going to be a problem, but I did not make a good decision. I drained the copier and brought it into his office which was in his house. He told me that he wanted it upstairs. I saw the flight of stairs and knew that this was going to be trouble. I told him to get the unit upstairs and I needed him to pull the handle up as I lifted the copier over each step. It had been raining outside and I was wearing a raincoat. We started up the steps and everything seemed to be going fine for about the first eight or nine steps. I then felt something burning on my legs. I looked down and I saw a stream of black liquid running down the front of my raincoat onto my legs and onto his white carpet. I immediately told him to stop and lowered the copier back down to the landing. I told him what had happened and asked him if I could call my boss and find out what to do. Bob told the customer that we would pay to have his carpet cleaned and that there should be no issues because the product cleans up nicely. The customer did not seem happy, but I assured him we would take care of it. I did not get to do the demonstration, and the customer told us that cleaning the carpet had not worked and got us to pay for all the new carpet for his complete set of stairs. He ended up buying a copier elsewhere. I should have known that my initial thoughts on this customer were correct and made him come to our office for a demonstration and had service install the machine after he bought it. The lesson I learned was to always prepare in advance for your demonstration, never wing it.

Chapter 16
Miss You Dad

In 1982, tragedy struck our family. My father had a heart attack that required triple bypass surgery. He was only 56 years old at the time. He was a bricklayer and had always appeared to be in the best of health. It turned out that there was a heredity issue in our family that he did not know about where we produce an excess amount of bad cholesterol. At the time statin drugs were not really in use. He ended up having to have a triple bypass to take care of the problem. A few months after the surgery he wanted to go back to work, but the bricklayer's union would not approve of his return to work. He seemed lost without work. He looked like a shadow of the strong man that I had come to love as a child. After he felt that he had recovered enough he started doing odd jobs on his own. Looking back at it now from my own experience, I realized that he had some form of Post Traumatic Stress Disorder (PTSD) as a by-product of his triple bypass surgery. Little did I know that 39 years later I would have a similar challenge. On August 17,1982, my father was building a stone water fountain for a local restaurant. He finished the job, swept up afterwards, put his broom against the wall and died. This would be the second and last time my father saved my life. Without us learning about the hereditary issue with cholesterol in our family, I probably would not have gotten tested for the same issue. I do have the same problem but am still here due to the improvements in medical technology and of course by knowing what caused my dad's heart issues. I miss my father greatly, and often hope that he looks down on Cindy and I and is proud of what we have accomplished during our lives.

Chapter 17
The Big Bang

Bob Bangert had left the company three years earlier to start his own business, and I was promoted to general manager from sales manager. While in that role, Bob reached out to me and offered to make me a partner in his business. Cindy and I seriously considered it and took the financials from Bob's new company to an accountant to determine if Bob's company was solvent enough to support him and I as we grew the company. The accountant said that it was possible but that it would require an extremely aggressive growth curve to hit the necessary targets needed. After hearing his feedback, we decided not to go into partnership with Bob. As it turned out it was the right move. Bob ended up selling his company about three years after he had left Gordon Flesch and moved up to northern Wisconsin. Not making the move to his new company proved to be the right decision. This was a splendid example of the path not taken.

In my new roll, as general manager, I was responsible for everything at the St. Charles branch of the company. We had a great office manager and an excellent service manager, so I tried to keep my focus on hiring the right salespeople so that we could continue to sustain good growth. I left the hiring of office personnel to my office manager and service hiring to our service manager. My service manager was an outstanding manager. His name was Jim Durkin. He stayed with the company for a few years after I left but he and the new general manager did not really agree completely. Jim was focused on doing whatever it took to keep the customer satisfied. Sometimes that path was more expensive than upper management felt was necessary. He was also great with his service technicians. He was always calm even in the most hectic situations. Jim Durkin is still a service manager for another dealership. Ironically, the dealership he now works for sells both Canon and Toshiba copiers.

Most of the salespeople I selected did a respectable job for us and we had little turnover. The ones who did leave usually left the industry. During my tenure, I hired a lot of good salespeople, who moved on to other companies as better opportunities arose. I cannot recall any who left our company and went to work for one of our competitors while I was the general manager. I remember one situation where one of my quick studies in sales left the company to go to medical school. I wished him luck, hopefully he became as good a doctor as he was a salesperson. Another one who decided to leave our company went into the family business which made large industrial rollers in Batavia, his name is John Bingham. John became the president of that company, and he was still there as of the last presidential election. I ran into him while working as an election judge, and I was happy that he still remembered me. He indicated that he had adapted a lot of his management style from me. I took that as a complement. My most memorable hiring was a salesperson named Stefan Borges. Stefan had beaten me on some sales when I was a sale representative. He worked for Ambassador. Ambassador was the name of the Canon branch. My first reaction to hiring him was to rule him out as a salesperson for us because he had beaten me. Then I remembered what I had been told by Ted Williams at GFC "always look for employees that can someday do your job." I hired Stefan and he did well for us. He won a Canon trip with us in his first year. I guess that it would be as close as you can get to Rookie of the Year in our business. Stefan was still with the company when I left Gordon Flesch.

Other than that chance meeting with John, I had not heard from any of my previous employees at Gordon Flesch until the strangest thing happened. I received a text just this year from my former nemeses after more than thirty years. The text was from Stefan Borges. Stefan and I had a history together on two fronts as competitors and as coworkers. When we were competitors, Ambassador would pitch that you should buy direct and cut out the middleman and we would pitch that we had a choice in what products we carried and that you would be working directly with the ownership not just some salesperson for a big company. Later of course he worked directly for me at Gordon Flesch.

In most cases I made the decisions on whom would be hired, but in one case I had a salesperson forced on me. He happened to be the owner's youngest son. My job was to teach him, like all the salespeople, the nuances of selling our product professionally. He did an excellent job as a salesperson initially, but being part of the family, he began to take liberties that would not be available to non-family members. I was told to just approve any expenses that the youngster might submit, and it would be approved in Wisconsin. Some of these expenses might be considered unusual from a business perspective. Little did I know that his arrival would alter my life from that day forward.

In late 1988, I was called into a meeting in my office with the President, Vice President, and CEO from the main location in Wisconsin. I knew this could not be good for all three of them to come down. I was informed that effective immediately, I would no longer be the general manager and that my job would be given to the owner's youngest son. I was given the option to take a couple of other lesser jobs in the company. I decided to accept a major account manager job with Gordon Flesch and told them that I wanted a $6,000 draw per month. I did the job for eight months while I was looking for another job. I beat my draw against commission every month over those last eight months and had met the criteria for the dealer trip. I then proceeded to walk into my former office and told the owner that I had just qualified for the trip. He congratulated me, and I told him that I was not done talking. I then told him that effective immediately, I quit. He told me that I would only be paid for orders that were already installed. I had anticipated that they would not pay me for orders that had not yet been installed. I gave the orders which had not been installed to other salespeople so they would get paid for them, even though I sold them. What I learned was that blood truly is thicker than water! This was my first experience with nepotism, but it would not be my last.

For many years I was anger over what had happened with me and Gordon Flesch, but looking at it now in retrospect, I know that it was the best thing that could have happened to me, because it opened my future to new opportunities that I would never have gotten had I stayed at Gordon Flesch.

After leaving Gordon Flesch Company initially, my choices of jobs were extremely limited. Gordon Flesch was not going to give me a referral and they were a big name in the copier market, so most manufacturers did not want to offend them by hiring an employee who had just quit. I ended up going to work for the only company that disliked Gordon Flesch as much as I did at the time. I went to work for Ambassador in a new position that they were creating. They wanted to have a dedicated facsimile sales team in each of their three offices. I was to be the manager of one of these locations. It took me a year at Ambassador to figure out that selling facsimile machines alone was not going to give me the opportunity or the income that I wanted in the copier industry. I decided that the only way I was going to be able to move up was to move over to direct sales to the dealerships that sold to companies. Now that I had been separated from Gordon Flesch for a time, I knew that I would be free to interview with various manufacturers. I had interviews with Ricoh, Panasonic, and Toshiba. I received three job offers and each one was unique. The key for Cindy and my future was for me to choose wisely on the next job. The Ricoh position was as regional parts manager, and it was my first choice. I thought it would combine my background in parts from the Army with what I had learned in the copier industry. I like the person in charge of the region and the job seemed remarkably interesting. Unfortunately, in the copier industry change is constant. The Regional Director that interviewed me and offered me the position got let go. Ricoh was "restructuring" the way they were going to manage parts management. This meant that the position I would have been taking no longer existed. I was lucky that this change occurred before I started with Ricoh, otherwise I would have had a noticeably short career with Ricoh. My next option was Panasonic as a District Sales Manager. I was familiar with their products from my time at Gordon Flesch, and knew some of the people that worked there, so it seemed like a logical choice. Little did I know what would happen next.

Chapter 18
Shortest Job in History

I knew that selling directly to dealerships, who in turn sold to end users would be completely different from what I had been doing for the last ten years, but I felt I was ready to move up. Panasonic and Toshiba both had made me offers to be a District Sales Manager. The person in charge of the region at Panasonic was a gentleman named Fred Eddy, and I had worked together in the past, so it seemed like a natural fit for me. Their corporate office was close to where Cindy and I lived and the territory at Panasonic was Illinois and Indiana, so I decided that I would take the Panasonic job.

I accepted the job at Panasonic and was told to report to their office in Elgin on June 1, 1990, for my new employee processing. I got my picture taken and my new badge from the personnel depart and I was now on board. I then watch one of the upper-level managers I would be working for get embarrassed in front of the office staff by his Japanese superior. I could not believe that Panasonic would treat a manager like that in front of the entire office staff. I decided at that second, that I could not work for a company that would publicly embarrass one of their employees in front of his subordinates. So, I made a split-second decision that impacted the next 30 years of my life. I walked back to the personnel department and told that, they might think I am crazy, but I have decided that I do not want to work for Panasonic. This all took place in less than an hour. It is not on my resume. It turned out to be one of the smartest decisions I have made in my life thus far.

I then replied to the job offer that I had gotten from Toshiba out of Irvine California, accepting their District Sales Manager position. The job did not pay quite as much as the Panasonic job, and the office was much farther away from home, but it felt like the best choice at that point. Little did I know that less than five years later Panasonic would close that regional office as they downsized. And that ten years later Panasonic would be out of the office equipment business, and I would have been out of work. Another twist of fate that turned out to be the right choice eventually. I guess you could say that the third time was the charm in this case.

Chapter 19
Toshiba and a Changing Culture

After deciding not to take the Panasonic job, I went to work a month later with Toshiba on July 1, 1990. I did not know it at the time, but I was one of several people who had been hired on that date across the entire country. In all, there were at least five District Sales Managers hired on that day with Toshiba. Toshiba had also just hired a new president named Richard Walker, and his goal was to change the culture at Toshiba. I was hired by the VP of Sales at the time. His name was Ron Milici. I was replacing a man named Mike Elrod, who had been promoted to a new role at the company as an Area Sales Manager (ASM). The ASM's job was to focus on recruiting new dealers in open territories throughout their assigned region. The ASM position would end up being short lived. There were only two people to hold the ASM job. Mike Elrod would be the first to fill this newly created position, but Mike left the company about a year later. He took a position with a local Toshiba copier dealership named Distinctive as the Vice President of Sales. The new ASM was a man named Joe Cannon. Joe had been a DSM for Ricoh and saw the ASM as an opportunity to move up in the copier industry. He would be the second and last person to fill the ASM role. The elimination of the ASM role in the company less than three years after it was started was one of the first of many changes that I saw when I was at Toshiba.

I learned later that I was not Ron's first choice. He had wanted someone with DSM experience, but he was overruled by someone. Later I was told that he had concerns that I might not make it as a District Sales Manager (DSM). Hearing that was all I needed for motivation to succeed. I only managed to last and thrive at Toshiba for the next thirty years. I guess Ron was wrong. Later he retired and was working part time on a golf course in California. Ironically, I saw five Toshiba presidents and six Toshiba vice-presidents come and go. Up until the time I joined Toshiba, the DSM had filled a different type of role. The old school DSMs were tasked with keeping the dealer's warehouse full and making sure the dealer owners were happy by taking them to dinner, entertainment, and copious drinking.

Dick Walker, the new president, saw the DSM's (District Sales Managers) role in a different light. He saw the need for the DSM to be more proactive in the dealerships they covered. He felt it was our job to help the dealership train their salespeople, help them recruit people, develop sell-through promotions, and help the dealers sell our products. Additionally, it was our role to attain the sales targets assigned to us and to our dealers. We also were tasked to recruit new dealers in markets that were underperforming and eliminate dealers who did not attain their sales targets from Toshiba. Dealers welcomed the new direction that Toshiba was going since it was helping them grow. They were not fond of being graded on their performance. Unfortunately, most of the old school DSMs could not or had no desire to adapt, so they ended up going the way of the dinosaurs. None of the old school DSMs who were with Toshiba in the Midwest, the day I started lasted more than a year after Mr. Walker's sweeping changes that started on July 1, 1990. These old school DSMs were just not ready to perform all the functions that were required in the new vision of the DSM position.

The first step in Mr. Walker's plan was to evaluate where each of our salespeople were regarding knowing our products. This started with a demonstration contest for all District Sales Managers on both the copier products and the newly added facsimile products. At that time Toshiba was divided into two zones. All the DSMs from the eastern zone were flown out to the zone office in Parsippany, New Jersey, The western region DSMs were flown out to the corporate office in Irvine, California to do a demonstration for the entire executive team. This demo contest happened within the first few months I was employed, so I was a little nervous, but since I had just stopped selling down the street, I was confident that I could do well. I ended up winning the demo contest for the entire eastern half of the country. A former Toshiba trainer who had been promoted to DSM won the contest in the western region. This was my first taste of success in my new job. I knew that I had made the right decision to go with Toshiba. Little did I know at the time that I would spend the rest of my working career with Toshiba.

The next phase of Dick's plan was to determine how well each of us knew our respective sales territory. He brought in an independent company to develop a boilerplate for analyzing each market in your territory. It was called the Primary Market Strategy or PMS for short. Everyone rolled their eyes at the acronym.

As it turned out, the study was very comprehensive. It covered market potential based on business index, required manpower that we should have in the area, present coverage by Toshiba, and all the major competitors in each market. We had two weeks to complete the research on our top three potential markets. We were then flown out to California to review our markets with the corporate team. None of us had done anything like this in the past, so we were all petrified doing the presentation. As it turned out the newer reps like me did well, and the old veterans did not. One of our sales team, a DSM named Bubba, was so shaken that we had to carry him back to the hotel. They tried to trip us up on the details of our presentation, but if you could support what you had presented with facts you were in good shape. We were frequently challenged by details in our presentations. Both the demo contest and the PMS presentation gave me all the confidence in the world that I could be one of the best DSMs in the company. Bubba would be the last of the three old school DSMs in the Midwest who were with the region when I started to leave the company. PMS was the last straw for him. He wanted something that was less stressful. He left the copier industry and started selling automotive software. It made all of us who knew him laugh at the thought of Bubba and software in the same sentence.

Chapter 20
Cleaning House

My initial territory with Toshiba was the state of Illinois. I had dealers in most of the larger markets, but Chicago was the key market, and it was a mess. There were six Toshiba dealers in the six counties that represent the Chicago market, but only two of them had the ability to grow and be successful with Toshiba. I had to clean up the market and find the right players if Toshiba and I were going to be successful and grow the business. To confirm my thoughts on the potential of all the dealers, based on the information I was given I needed to meet with each of the dealers. These meetings confirmed my suspicions about the potential of each dealer. Monitoring the dealer network was like a minefield. Most dealers were entrepreneurs, who had grown their business from nothing. A few were second or even third generation owners, whose parents or grandparents had started the business. Although they grew their businesses in diverse ways, they all had one thing in common. They all made up their own set of rules as to what was right or wrong regarding their sales. Typically, if it was good for them, it was right. The one thing all the successful dealers had in common was their unique approach to how to run a successful business. On the other hand, as someone who worked for the manufacturer, we often had to make decisions that were for the greater good. My job for the next thirty years was to navigate this minefield and make the right decisions.

Each of the dealers I needed to remove from the market still had some value. In the short-term losing them would cost Toshiba some revenue, but to grow the Chicago market the right way, I had to do what was necessary. It was time for me to make decisions on each dealer and when they should be terminated. I had to make the correct choice on each dealer. To understand the nature of our dealers I will illustrate some examples in the various markets. I will go through the most noteworthy "cheaters." The Toshiba dealer contract specifically stated your assigned geography and the fact that you could not make products available to another party for resale, whether that be machines or supplies. Each dealer signed an agreement that says they will only sell Toshiba equipment and supplies within their assigned geography, and that those sales are only to end-users and not for resale. Over my thirty years with Toshiba, I was amazed and how dealers would stretch the rules as to sell our products. The cases below are ones that occurred while I was still new as a DSM. I was very naïve at the time. Over the years, I would have to correct many dealers for their creative marketing approach with our products.

The first violator involved a dealer who was from a country in the far east. Her dealership would buy equipment and ship that equipment out of the country through an import/export company owned by her brother. She denied that she was doing anything in violation of her contract. I was able to prove that units were leaving the United States and terminated her dealership. This resulted in a loss of hardware revenue for Toshiba and me, but I had committed to making the right choices to grow the market. This dealer of course complained, but did not cause any repercussions, because she knew it was illegal and taking it to court would cause her more problems than it would solve. She took on another product line, which was probably willing to look the other way and continue her practice exporting copy machines. This was my first taste of nepotism in the copier industry, but it would not be my last.

The next case involved two dealers doing something similar with Toshiba supplies. Supplies and parts are the lifeblood of the copier industry. Look at the copier itself as the razor and supplies and parts as the blades. Being a copier dealer was attractive to young entrepreneurs because of the three revenue streams. The copier sales, the toner sales, and the maintenance contract on the copiers. In the copier industry there are lots of companies that sell alternative supplies for Toshiba products. A lot of these supplies were counterfeit and could damage the machines when they are used in our copiers. The thing that these third-party companies want the most is genuine Toshiba supplies. They could not buy them directly from Toshiba, so their best sources were to find Toshiba dealers who were willing to sell them genuine supplies. Here is how it was done. The authorized Toshiba dealer would buy more supplies than they needed for their customer base and sell the excess to the third-party companies. These dealers were caught easily because Toshiba had formulas that charted what the norm was for every type of machine's usage of supplies. If the dealer was far outside the norm, we would meet with them and warn them about the suspected abuse. It would stop some of the abuse, but not the big offenders. They were much more creative. The two dealers in question were so far out of tolerance that we knew they were reselling toner. What they were doing was selling the toner to third party companies who in turn sold or traded generic supplies to the dealer. If the third-party company got the supplies in trade, they would then undercut the pricing that our loyal dealers were using for their customers. The end user was getting genuine supplies at a lower price, so they were none the wiser. The cheating dealers who received generic toner in trade which they would then use in their machines. This allowed them to make money twice on supplies. The generic toner did not work as well as the genuine Toshiba toner, so we had an excess number of complaints from customers who were being serviced by the dealer in question. I terminated both their dealerships for violating their dealer contract after repeated warnings. The larger of the two dealers threatened to sue us for wrongful termination but his attorney told him that it would be a frivolous lawsuit, and he backed off. Ironically, the owner of the larger two dealers passed away about a year after I terminated his dealership, and the new owner asked to become a Toshiba dealer again, but I declined their offer.

The fourth dealer was the most difficult to catch. He had a relative who was also a copier dealer in the market with another copier brand. Yet another encounter with nepotism in our industry. He would sell or trade Toshiba products to this other dealership so that they both could offer their customers an alternative product at a higher price, or in some cases the non-Toshiba dealer would sell them our product and have his brother's dealership do the service. This of course was collusion which is illegal. Once I threatened to terminate his dealership, he tried a new tactic. He reported me to the Vice President of Sales, stating that I did not know what his dealership was doing because I never visited his dealership. Fortunately, I was meticulous about sending out follow-up letters to each of my dealers, recapping my last visit with them in detail. I produced copies of the letters to my boss showing the last four visits to this dealer in the last eight months. My boss said this was all he needed to know the dealer was not telling the truth. We then started the termination process with his dealership. Little did I know that this would trigger a strange twist in the market. It turned out that one of the other Toshiba dealers named Copier Dynamics offered to buy this fourth dealership. I am confident that he sold because he knew that he would be terminated, and the value of his dealership would not be worth as much if the dealership had been cancelled. The two companies combined and became Advanced Business Technologies (ABT). So, this termination works out better than could be expected. I eliminated one dealer I was trying to get rid of and strengthened one of my other dealers in the same market. I could not have asked for a better outcome at the time. ABT was owned by a gentleman from New York. His name was Harry Talanian. Harry was a great guy and had kept some of the good salespeople from the other dealership. The newfound company did a respectable job for Toshiba for several years. Eventually, Harry decided he wanted to retire, and he sold his business to Toshiba. It became Toshiba Business Solutions-Illinois. The sale of ABT to Toshiba was not received well by the two large Toshiba dealers in the market. They felt that it would negatively impact their sales. They both began to diversify the brands of products that they offered to their customers to protect their dealerships. I do not believe this was solely the reason for the diversification of products by the dealers, but it had clearly impacted on their feelings about Toshiba.

There was one other dealer I had to remove. They did not fit the norm for an underproducing dealer. This dealer had a branch office in Chicago but was headquartered in Wisconsin. Camadon was a large dealership, but did not sell much Toshiba products in Chicago, so we decided that it would be beneficial for us to sever our relationship with them. I decided to set up a meeting with the owner of that company personally in their office in Wisconsin. Since this dealer was headquartered in Wisconsin, we could not cancel them because Wisconsin has franchise laws to protect the dealer. However, we did have the right to remove the Illinois counties from their agreement. I decided to bring my service manager John Rauwolf along as a witness and to provide moral support. I told the dealer that we would like to remove the Illinois counties from their contract. And since we would be removing some counties from their contract, we would allow them to return boxed Toshiba inventory. We asked if we could go through their warehouse and take pictures of their Toshiba inventory, so that we could determine what they could return to us. The dealer went ballistic, he threatened to throw us out of his dealership. He then had us escorted out and we never met with him again. In fact, we were removed so quickly that we did not even get a chance to grab our boots. It was the middle of winter when we made this visit. I was so glad that I had made the decision to bring my service manager with me on the call. After the call he thanked me profusely for getting him thrown out of dealership. He said it was the first time it had ever happened to him, and he had been with Toshiba for twenty years at the time. It was also my first time, but I did not know if my last time would not be. Ironically, the dealer was so mad that he decided to punish us by stopping selling Toshiba all together. My decision to visit him and approach him directly had worked out as I hoped. Mr. C. ended up selling his dealership to another entity in the Milwaukee market not long after he had resigned as a Toshiba dealer. My decision to end this relationship was a good decision, but we would get another unexpected benefit of this resignation by Camadon.

Chapter 21
New Beginnings

Eventually, I got the market down to two of the original dealers and decided to add one new dealer to the market now that it had been cleaned up. I had been impressed with one of the former executives of Camadon and heard he might be looking to start his own dealership. Rich Cucco had a reputation of being extremely aggressive so I had to be concerned about how my other two dealers would take to having Rich in the market. If I made the decision to bring him on board as a Toshiba dealer, it would be an incredibly risky move on my part. I met him in a large empty building in Lake County. He was currently starting out his new business in his father's garage. I was very skeptical at first until he started to go over his business plan. He told me that he would not only grow the dealership, but that he would become the largest Toshiba dealer in the market in a few years and one of the top dealers in the country. I do not know why I believed him, but my gut told me he would do it. I also felt that starting out as a small startup would help to mitigate the impact he would have on my other dealers. When I told them I was adding a new dealership to the market they were not happy, but they accepted the fact and did not do anything radical. Now all I had to do was to get my Regional Manager to agree with me that adding Imagetec was an innovative idea. Fortunately, I was able to sell him on the addition. I brought Imagetec on as a dealer in 1991. Once he was on board, the market started to grow right away. Rich's aggressive approach to the market generated more competition, which created more Toshiba sales. The changes I made in the Chicago market worked, and

I learned a valuable lesson. Sometimes it is best to go with your gut. Adding Imagetec was one of the smartest decisions I made as a DSM. It was a tremendous risk, but it had worked out. I gained a dedicated Toshiba dealer for several years and kept the conflict with my other dealers to a minimum. Rich's new company was to be called Imagetec. Over the years he would grow the company just as he had projected. They would become one of the largest Toshiba dealers in the Midwest and the whole country. He won several Toshiba sales contests for dealer trips, but the high point would be when his dealership was named dealer of the year in 2004. He was presented the award on our dealer trip while we were in Russia. I also designed his territory to include the northern counties of the Chicago market so that it would not be a complete overlap with Distinctive's sales area since they were headquartered in the southern suburbs in Alsip, Illinois.

Rich Cucco Dealer of the Year-Russia

Distinctive Business Products had been a Toshiba dealer before I started with Toshiba and had slowly been growing their business. Two men owned it initially, but Joe Mozeki, the other owner decided to leave the business and sold his share of the company to his partner John Cosich. John and Joe had been a salespeople for Xerox in their past lives and had started

Distinctive Business Product on their own. Starting a dealership from scratch is difficult, but he had done a respectable job up to that time. He also had brought in a consulting firm to help him structure the company for growth now that he was the sole owner. The consultant told him to grow, you must have levels of management so you can add more salespeople. This is when they added Mike Elrod. Since Mike had been with Toshiba before Distinctive Business Products his joining Distinctive was a major help for us. We were able to build several extremely large purchases together to help Distinctive grow. John's dealership would continue to grow for several more years. He eventually sold the business but came back into the market a few years later with a new company called Proven Business Products. The name came from one of his sons who told him that he had already proven that he could build a business, and the name stuck. Over the years, they continued to win many Toshiba trips over the years.

Chapter 22
Just the Fax

The Toshiba product line was very dated in the early 90's. We had a mix of three generations of products, so there was no uniformity as to how the products looked or functioned. With our aggressive pricing approach and proven reliability of our products we were still able to grow and compete in the market. I ended up winning three trips with Toshiba while I was a DSM in my first four years. I also was the top DSM in the country twice. None of my success as a DSM could have occurred if I had not made the right decision on what to do in the Chicago market. If I had not cleaned up the market, I am confident that my career at Toshiba would have been short lived. Sometimes a decision you make can have a much greater impact than you originally expected.

Toshiba made another marketing change in early 1990. Toshiba decided that the facsimile division could not survive with the limited revenue that it generated due to low margins and a limited product line. It needed to be part of a more profitable division. They decided that they should merge the facsimile division with the copier division. This was a great decision by Toshiba. We were a natural fit for the fax products. However, this meant integrating more people and more territory changes. I went from having territory that included all of Illinois to a territory that was now the greater Chicago market and Wisconsin. Since two of the former DSM's had already left the company, we were able to integrate the people from the fax division seamlessly. There were two DSMs from the fax division, who were offered positions in the Midwest, only one of them accepted a position as a DSM with us. Her name was

Michele Cockins. Prior to her being part of the fax division with Toshiba, she had a background in copiers from her days at Xerox. She was an outstanding hire and was a long-term employee of Toshiba. In fact, she is still with Toshiba as of 2024 and is now a Director for Toshiba working closely with the Toshiba Business Solutions locations. She was also one of my fiercest rivals when we were both DSMs and was one of my staunchest supporters once I assumed the role of Regional Sales Manager and later Regional Director for the Midwest.

Shortly after the facsimile division became part of the Toshiba Copier Division, a decision to streamline our division was made by eliminating the Government Manager positions across the country. The Midwest had two of these GEM managers. One decided to leave Toshiba and the other assumed one of the vacant DSM positions that had been created with the newest alignment. His name is Brian Kohn. Brian had been a GEM DSM. His previous position was eliminated. So, in late 1990, he became a DSM for Toshiba. He had a very unusual territory in that he covered southern Indiana and Illinois except for the greater Chicagoland area which stayed as part of my territory along with Wisconsin. This turned out to be a great learning experience for him because he had not worked as a DSM before. This allowed him to receive some firsthand experience with our dealer's day-to-day operations. Brian did so well when Toshiba made the next change of assignment and added a new Regional Government Education and Major Account Manager position. Brian was promoted to that role in 1992. He now had a huge territory to cover. His territory covered the eastern half of the United States. He is still with Toshiba and is currently the longest tenured salesperson at Toshiba with over 35 years with the company. I worked closely with Brian for over 29 years. He grew tremendously through his tenure at Toshiba. Toshiba was his first job in the copier business. I guess you could say that he and Toshiba both made a wise decision in making him one of their employees.

Chapter 23
We Didn't Start the Fire

In the meantime, I had another market that needed to be fixed. It was an underperforming market that covered both the Springfield market and the Decatur market in southern Illinois. I set up a meeting with the owners. It would be my first visit to their location. Because they were in a rather remote location, they were not used to seeing a Toshiba DSM visit them. The owners were a married couple named Chuck and Sherry Krull. I did not know what roles each of them performed in the dealership. And since I was new to the DSM role, I assumed that they were equal partners in the company. I also assumed that Chuck ran the sales side of the company, and Sherry managed the administrative side. Boy was I wrong! As soon as I started to review their performance, indicating that they were underperforming, Sherry went ballistic. Chuck never said a word during my entire visit. However, his wife talked plenty. She then unleased a string of obscenities toward me that would make a sailor blush. After that she proceeded to let me know that they would sell what they could and that if that was not enough, I was free to find someone else. She then threw me out of their office. When I got back to Chicago, and told my RSM about my experience, he laughed and told me that he should have told me that Sherry has quite a temper, and that she was the more outspoken of the two owners. If I had that information prior to my call, I probably would have approached the visit differently. Ironically, a few days later Sherry called me and apologized for the outburst, and that they would welcome any ideas I had that could help sell more of our products. She even sent a letter to the RSM at the time and apologized to us as a region. Since they were the best option within the market, we kept them on board as Toshiba dealers.

A few months later we experienced a territory change and they were no longer my dealer. They eventually sold their dealership to an upcoming mega dealer called Danka. They were Danka's first purchase of a dealer in the Midwest. Danka went on to be such a large mega dealer that they partnered with Toshiba for many years selling products for us, and at one time were Toshiba's largest dealer in the country. In fact, Toshiba bought all of Danka's assets in South America over the years. Danka in turn sold the rest of their company in 2008. They sold their remaining total assets to Konica Minolta for 240 million dollars. The presence of mega dealers like Danka, IKON, and Marco launched a new chapter in our approach to dealers. Little did any of us know how great an impact the mega dealer concept would have on our industry. Eventually, this led to several mega dealers buying dealers in various markets and manufacturers buying dealers in key markets to protect their base. This was a perfect example of how one minor change could impact so many companies and so many people.

Chapter 24
Didn't See That One Coming!

C hange is usually a good thing, but knowing the right time to make a change is a great thing. Earlier in my career, when I was selling Canon copiers at Gordon Flesch company in about 1986 Canon introduced a product called the IM-30 which was their first digital copier. It was supposed to connect to up to four printer units so that it could copy and print at 120 pages per minute. It had only one problem, no printer interface ever became available for the product, so it did not sell well. This was the perfect example of being too early to market a product. In the early 1990's, other manufacturers began to introduce "digital" copiers, but they all lacked connectivity. All that changed in 1996. Ricoh introduced the Imagio MF200 digital copier. Others like Canon and Konica followed with their own digital products with connectivity. Products with names like Aficio and Imagio. It seemed like with this new connected technology you had to give your product a strange new name.

DP-2460 Digital Copier

Unfortunately, Toshiba did not time their entry into the connected digital copier market well. Toshiba did not introduce their first connected digital copier until December 1997. The new Toshiba digital copier was called the DP-2460. It had an optional controller (SC-1) that allowed it to connect to the customers network, but the SC-1 was extremely expensive, and the controller was a bulky external device. It was also not part of a complete product line. This was almost eighteen months after the other major manufacturers jumped into the digital market. The good news was that not all customers were anxious to change to digital products which were more expensive than analog copiers at the time. Toshiba aggressively priced our analog products which allowed us to compete in the interim, but the damage was already done. Toshiba had misread how rapidly the market would change from analog to digital and it cost all of us. This one decision led to many of our single line Toshiba dealers adding a second product line during the time that we lacked a digital offering. Those dealers felt they needed to have a digital offer as an alternative for their customers.

In 2001 Toshiba completely joined the digital fray. We now had the beginning of a full line with a funny name! Toshiba launched the "e-Studio" line. We were told it meant a place where art is made. The first of these products was the e-Studio 35. It was offered with an option network interface that allowed it to be scanner, a copier, and a printer. We even had a program to give the interface away for free with any Toshiba lease. The new e-Studio products were a tremendous success. Over the next twelve months, it was followed by a series of digital products that allowed us to compete on a level playing field with other manufacturers with up to sixty-five prints or copies per minute. Although this was not a decision that I made, it is an example of how one decision can impact so many companies and so many people. Thousands of people at dealerships and Toshiba were impacted by this one decision on when to enter the connected digital market.

Chapter 25
European Vacation

In 1995 something happened that could have ended my story. When I started as a DSM with Toshiba DSMs could win the right to go on the dealer trip. This slowly changed over the years as increased money saving programs were put into play. By 1996 it had been restricted to RSM and above. Toshiba had always been famous for their dealer trips as being over the top as far as how lavish they were. In this case they chartered an entire high end cruise ship. The ship was the Seabourn Pride (below). This trip went from Rome to Sicily and then back to Rome. The trip included our top eighty dealers and their significant others. It also included Toshiba upper management level people and some mid-level managers who had won this incentive trip and their wives for a total of two hundred people. On the last night of the cruise, we were returning to Rome to travel back to the United States. At about two in the morning the ship's fire alarms started going off. The crew had already started contacting each cabin to advise everyone that this was not a drill. We were told to put on our life jackets and to go to our lifeboat stations. We had no idea what was happening, but we could smell diesel fuel burning. As it turns out, two of the ships' four diesel engines had caught fire. It appeared that we would soon be told to abandon ship. The captain had requested other ships in the area to come to our rescue should the lifeboats be lowered. Fortunately, fate was on our side and the crew was able to put out the fire. Had the fire not been caught early and it extinguished who knows what might have happened to all of us. I am not a person who believes in triskaidekaphobia, but if I did this was surely a splendid example. This was my wife's and my thirteenth cruise, and it was on July 13th that the fire occurred. Thank goodness it was a Thursday not Friday, or the ship might have sunk! Looking back at the event it was interesting to remember what all the different people had with them when they got up on deck and what they elected to wear. There were people in formal wear still up from partying all night. Others were in bathrobes, and some in even less. If only cellphones with cameras had been in vogue at that time. We would have been a huge hit on Facebook. I was simply happy to be able to get back to the port safely. The thought of drowning at sea was and still is one of my worst nightmares.

Seaborne Pride

The next year while on another Toshiba trip that included a visit to Paris, we had one of the most unique experiences of our time together. My wife and I, plus another couple who had been on the trip, decided that we should see a little bit more of Paris so we decided that we should do something that would be a once-in-a-lifetime experience. Michele Cockins and her husband Steve were the other couple. Michele spoke a little French, so she somehow got us a reservation to have dinner in the Eiffel Tower. This was unheard of without reservations months in advance, but we got a reservation for the same day. We had a fantastic dinner at the Jules Verne restaurant (below) which is about one hundred feet up in the Eiffel Tower. Once we left, something that could have been disastrous occurred. There was a bicycle race in progress that was going around the tower and through the city. We hailed a cab, and he drove up quickly to the tower to pick the four of us up. He was in a hurry to pick us up and get going so he could beat the bicycle traffic. In fact, he was so much in a hurry that he nearly killed my wife! As we were all getting into the cab, he decided to take off, even though Cindy was not completely inside the cab. We all started shouting for him to stop but he did not speak English. Michele finally shouted at him "Arretez la Voiture" or "Stop the Car!" in French and he finally stopped the cab. Cindy was able to get in without any injuries, but this could have been a fatal accident. To this day, we all still remember that dinner and the unique and near disastrous ending.

Jules Verne Restaurant-Eiffel Tower

Chapter 26
Who's on First

During my four plus years as a District Sales Manager with Toshiba, I had three different Regional Sales Manager. The first one, who was the Region Sales Manager (RSM) when I was hired, was terminated for cause. I do not know what the cause was, but he never worked in the industry again. The second one was a man named Steve Hughes. He had been on the service team within the Toshiba organization and had transferred to sales. He did not work well with the DSMs in the Midwest Region to put it mildly. He lasted for about a year and then took another job with Lanier. The third one was a gentleman named Mike Bittel. Mike had been a DSM in the eastern region and was promoted to the Regional Sales Manager position. Mike and I got along very well, he was also ex-military. He was a very down-to-earth guy and an excellent decision maker. I learned a lot from him. Unfortunately, he had lost interest in the copier business and working for someone else, so he left and bought a company making wooden trusses for housing in his hometown in Pennsylvania in 1995.

All this turnover of RSMs put the upper manager in a position where they did not want to bring in the wrong person, so they decided to take it slowly in recruiting a replacement. In the meantime, the Midwest team was operating without a leader. Our team was doing so well that we were leading the country in sales. It was time for Toshiba to make another change. They could not have the region that was doing the best finish first, it would have sent the wrong message out to the other regions. In the meantime, we also experience the elimination of two levels of managers to reduce costs. The two-zone concept was eliminated, which got rid of the Zone Managers, and it was decided that the DSMs should be recruiting dealers along with the RSMs, so the Area Sales Manager position was also eliminated. This allowed Toshiba to cut six managers across the country. Toshiba now had moved to a much flatter hierarchy. We now had five regions. Each of which had a RSM position that reported directly to the VP of Sales. While all this was going on we still had no RSM to replace Mike Bittel in the Midwest.

After few months, the Vice President of Sales, Tod Pulsifer, said he was receiving pressure from the President to get a new RSM on board. He gave us an ultimatum, either someone from the region takes the position or he had a candidate from the outside. The Midwest team of DSMs consisted of four DSMs. Two of which are still with Toshiba, the third went back to Pennsylvania and started his own dealership after a couple of years, and me. None of us really wanted the job because we were all doing well as DSMs and saw how there was a lot more turnover, in the RSM position, than in our positions. Not to mention more pressure and more responsibility. After much prompting from my fellow DSMs, everyone decided that I should apply for the RSM position. Tod agreed, and I moved into my new role as the RSM for the Midwest region. Little did I know that I would be taking a step backwards in pay. This is when I learned that upward mobility could come at some financial cost. It turned out that a top performing DSMs made more money than a starting RSM. No one told me that when I agreed to take the job. Tod promised that he would fix this discrepancy and true to his word he fixed it over the next two years. I received four pay increases during that time and was then making more than I would have as DSM. I was hoping that taking this new job was the right move, and that fate had put me in the right situation to lead a team. As it turns out, the person who would have taken the role as the RSM for Midwest came from another manufacturer. He ended up taking the same role as the RSM for the Western Region. His name was John Fahey, and he was more than happy to take the RSM role in the west instead of the Midwest. He did not have to relocate so it was good for him. He and I became rivals for several years, but he left the company after a few years and took a position with Konica Minolta. So, I guess I made the right decision for the Midwest Sales team. Had I not taken the job as the RSM, it is hard to tell how my future with Toshiba would have turned out. I am confident that I would not have stayed their long term, and my future would have been altered. Taking the RSM position at Toshiba was one of my best choices in my life.

Chapter 27

So, You Wanted to Be in Charge

The year was 1996 and I now had six people reporting to me four DSMs and two indirect reports who were Government Education Managers (GEM). My philosophy in my new role was to lead by example, always be fair, protect your team, and always tell the truth. I had learned a lot selling down the street and tried to apply what I had learned in the past to how I approached my new job. My region went on to be one of the best regions in the country every year. I was immensely proud of the group. Two members of the original team moved up into higher level positions with Toshiba and were still there in 2024. Over the next few years, I had to hire several additional people as the regions changed. Four of those additional salespeople stayed with Toshiba for at least 20 years. This type of longevity is unheard of in the office equipment industry, so it is one of the things I was most proud of during my time at Toshiba.

My four plus years as a DSM with three different RSMs had taught me a lot. I saw good points in each of my predecessors that I could use in my new role. I learned that one of the keys to success was to try and have the right people in place on your team. I needed to add one DSM for an open territory that had been created and an RGEM (Regional Government Education and Medical Manager) to cover the newly added part of my territory. These would be my first attempts at hiring in my new role at Toshiba. If only I had listened to myself about what type of individuals were needed for these two separate roles.

As I indicated, Toshiba was always realigning territories. When I started with Toshiba the country was divided into two zones and within the two zones there was a total of five regions. The next change occurred in 1997 when I received a call from the VP of Sales Tod Pulsifer to advise me that he was getting ready to announce that they would be closing the Central region office and going to just four regions. This change came less than a year after I had assumed the RSM role. He told me that his intent was to eliminate all the positions and realign the territories so that the states covered by the central region would be broken up and added to the other regions. As it is related to the Midwest region, we gained six states and lost one. I now had seventeen states for the rest of my time that I was at Toshiba. Tod told me that I would need an additional DSM, and did I have any interest in any of the DSMs that were currently in the central region. He asked me about one DSM in particular who had covered some of the northern states in what the central region was. Four of those states that were covered by that DSM were to become part of the new Midwest region. The DSM in question was Todd Lee. I had seen some of Todd's work in some presentations he had created on his own and circulated to others in the company. This told me that not only was he creative, but also unselfish by sharing what he had made with other DSMs. I decided that adding Todd to my dream team was a promising idea. It was a good decision on Tod Pulsifer's part to give me the option to add Todd Lee. He worked for me for several years after that and was a major contributor to our region. He left my region for a position as a general manager at one of our Toshiba Business Solutions (TBS) subsidiary locations in Minnesota. If I had not elected to make Todd part of my team when the Central Region was dissolved. Todd would never have become the general manager of Toshiba Business Solutions in Minnesota. This would have impacted not only him but also the one hundred people he would go on to manage at TBS-MN. Who knows where his path would have taken him, but it would have been dramatically different.

The first person I had to hire was for a DSM role to cover

the states in the Southwest part of our region that I had picked up in the recent elimination of the Central Region. Todd Lee would cover part of the fresh territory. He would manage North Dakota, South Dakota, Nebraska, and Minnesota, all states he had covered previously when he was in the Central Region. The southern portion of the territory which consisted of Missouri, Kansas, and the southern part of Ohio at the time was the area I needed to address. I interviewed several people for the position, but none of them were interested in relocating to Missouri. Toshiba required that you live in your territory at the time. I was up to my last possible candidate for the position. His name was Douglas Bastille. He happened to live in Central Missouri and worked for a small copier dealership in that area. I thought he would be a good fit at the time. I was wrong. It turned out that it did not take a lot of money to live in the area he was from, so he was not overly aggressive in his approach to success, to put it mildly. I got him up to speed on our products and told him what I wanted him to do. I wanted him to start out by meeting all his dealers in person. I went with him for the first couple of visits, and things went OK. The dealers were happy to have someone local. I then told him the next three dealers I wanted him to visit and to set up a schedule for those visits. A few days later I received my first call from one of the dealers who I told him to visit. They told me that he did not show up for the meeting he had set up with the dealer. I reached out to him to find out what the deal was, and he told me that he had a personal matter come up. I advise him that if something like that happens again, let me know and contact the dealer with a new date. He said he understood. The next week the same thing happened with another dealer. I asked Douglas again why he missed another visit. He told me that his wife was ill and that he had to take her to the doctor. When I asked why he had not called the dealer or me, he told me that he was just getting ready to make those calls. I started wondering if I had hired the right person. I decided to dig deeper into what the issue was on the first visit. He then told me the truth, which was that he had to help his friend at his old dealership and that they were interested in selling their dealership. I told him that it was not acceptable and that if I received another call from one of his dealers about a missed visit that I would have to write him up. He told me he understood. The next week, he reached out to me and told me that he had decided that the DSM job was not for him, and that he was going to go into partnership with his friend at the small dealership. All of this occurred in about ninety days. At least he saved me from the trouble of firing him. I learned a valuable lesson in that you should not hire out of desperation, because you probably will not be happy with the results. So, it was back to square one. I still needed a DSM for that area.

Meanwhile, I had secured a new Regional Government Education and Major Account Manager (RGEM) for the new area a few months earlier. He was the first person I had hired for a RGEM role. He seemed to be a perfect fit. His name was Wilhelm Schultz. He had reached out to me several times over the last few months and told me that he was looking to change from his current Regional Sales Manager (RSM) with another manufacturer. He said he had landed a huge major account in for this other manufacturer, and that they were not paying him what he thought he should get for the account. I thought that if he had already had success in with major accounts in the market, I wanted him to cover that I could not possibly go wrong. I thought that anyone who came after a job as aggressively as he had must be able to sell. I did not know that Wilhelm had a nickname that indicated his focus was on big dollar business. He was only interested in working large accounts and did not have time for the smaller GEM accounts. Wilhelm would make a great first impression with potential new accounts. He would promise all kinds of things, but did not follow through on delivering what he promised. I had made up my mind to put Wilhelm on probation when he told me that he could not stay at Toshiba because he was having health issues. So, he resigned before I could fire him.

Fortunately, on both hires I had sent them out to California for second interviews so that my boss could approve them before we hired them. I am sure that if it had been solely me decided on them, Toshiba probably would have thought that I was not very good at evaluating salespeople and have demoted me or let me go. I was now zero for two in the recruiting process.

I finally got it right on my next attempt at recruiting. He was a unique hire. His name was Kennedy Cross. Kennedy seemed to have a knack for being in the right place at the right time when opportunities presented themselves. He was a product trainer for Mita (later Kyocera) at the time that I interviewed him. Things were not going well for Mita at the time, and Kennedy decided he should start looking for a new job. His intuition was right. The day after I met with him and offered him a job, Mita declared bankruptcy. I decided that I would go back to the basics when hiring people for my region. Here is what I would be looking for in a sales employee. I wanted people who knew products and had trained others, had sold downstreet, or had service training on copiers. These are people who I thought would want to continue to grow. Fortunately, my new formula for the type of person I wanted was correct. Kennedy became the first of many successful hires. I brought him on board as a DSM to start with to cover an area that had just been vacated by someone who left for another company. One of the things that always stood out with Kennedy was his willingness to embrace new opportunities. Positions at Toshiba changed quite often, and Kennedy was always up for the challenge of a new role. Unfortunately, some of these new roles did not last long and I would find a way to bring Kennedy back to the team. During my time with Toshiba, Kennedy held four distinct positions, all as a part of the Midwest region either directly or indirectly. He stayed with Toshiba for over twenty years and just recently took a job as the Vice President of Sales at a large dealership in Indiana. I wish him well. I am sure he will do remarkable things.

I still needed to fill my Southwest DSM position. A substantial portion of my success as a Regional Sales Manager, and later as a Region Director, was due to hiring the right people. Hiring at the manufacturers level was completely different than hiring at the dealership level. With the manufacturers' level you had to know if the person you were hiring could work well on their own and fit in well with the team. People's skills and the desire to work hard were paramount. On my first DSM hire, and my first RGEM hire, I had chosen poorly. I hired someone who had been with a manufacturer before and seemed to have great people skills. Both of those first two hires turned out to not be focused on working hard or growing the business in their respective territories. They were more focused on just coasting along without doing additional work to help grow the Toshiba market share. Ironically, both Douglas and Wilhelm left Toshiba and went back to Missouri. Douglas to his small dealership with his brother, and Wilhelm just to go home. Their departures turned out to be two of the best decisions that I did not have to make.

In recruiting a replacement DSM for Douglas, I decided to go with someone who had the background I was planning to use going forward. My second DSM hire was a home run. His name was Paul Cox. Paul was a former salesperson for a Sharp dealership, but also had service experience with copiers. I knew from my own experience as a DSM that copier dealers really appreciate someone supporting them who knows the ins and outs of copier products. Additionally, he was a seven-year Navy veteran. I felt that based on his military background he would be very organized. He was a great hire over the years. He had many successes with Toshiba and worked for me for over twenty years before he retired. Over the years Paul and I found that we have had numerous similarities in our backgrounds and previous life experiences. I had now filled my vacant western territory.

Paul was not afraid to take chances to grow the business in his major markets. Paul's key markets were St. Louis and Kansas City. He was particularly good at setting up meetings with the various key dealers in the markets. The first tremendous success we had in St. Louis came from Paul setting up a meeting with to ex-employees of a company called IKON. IKON was one of the up-and coming mega dealers. These two gentlemen, Mike Golinaux and Dave Wilson, had no product line and one of them had a non-compete contract from their former employer. We met them in what appeared to be an old theater. There were all kinds of props laying around the area we met them in. However, Paul and I saw immense potential in them and a desire to become successful. All dealer applications had to go through the Regional Sales Manager/Director. I made the decision that we should give them a chance and bring them on as a dealer. They started out by buying a small former Toshiba dealer to give them a base and then proceeded to grow their dealership by attacking the school market. This was the fastest way for them to grow their business quickly. Toshiba was exceptionally good at being aggressive on pricing for bids and we started winning these bids with our new dealer called Document and Network Technology (DNT). Within ten years they grew their business from zero to ten million dollars. They continued to grow their business over the five years at a tremendous pace. Ultimately, Dave sold half of the business to Mike. He had decided that he had had enough of the copier industry. Mike continued to grow the business and sold the business to Marco in 2016. Marco is one of the large Mega dealers who is strategically purchasing dealers throughout the United States and St. Louis was a key market for them. DNT had grown their business to over twenty million dollars and had over 3,400 customers when they sold to Marco. And they had become one of Toshiba's largest dealers and one of our best successes in the Midwest. They were won of our top trip winners when we took our dealers to Spain in 2016. We saw a blank canvas in DNT, and what they could be with proper support. DNT was instrumental in my being the top RSM and later Regional Director in the country on several occasions. I made great decisions in my hiring of both Kennedy and Paul (below). They became two of my longest tenured employees and worked very well together. Here they are featured at a customer event after hours and still working hard.

Paul & Kennedy supporting Hotz, our dealer.

Paul and I had fixed one of our major markets in St. Louis but still had a glaring hole in our coverage in Kansas City. We had prospected every dealer in the market and called on several of them repeatedly. Finally, in 2003, one of the Kyocera/Mita dealers who Paul had known when he sold facsimile for Mita was interested in talking to us. We went out and met with him, but he was more interested in selling his dealership than becoming a dealer. One of the owners had sold out to his partner and the other one was in poor health. While working on the Mita/Kyocera dealer, we decided to also call on the large Minolta dealer in the market again. Konica and Minolta had merged in 2003, and Minolta dealers were not enamored with the new direction. The current owner was a man named R. D. Kerley. Hotz had been in the office equipment business for over sixty years. R. D. like what we presented to them and signed up as a dealer with Toshiba. Initially Paul and I were ecstatic, we finally had the dealer we needed in Kansas City. About three weeks after we signed them up as a dealer, we were told that Hotz and the Kyocera/Mita dealer had both decided to sell to Toshiba. They were to form what was called Toshiba Business Solutions Missouri Kansas (TBS-MO KS). The new president would be a gentlemen named Steve McCluhan. Steve was a former employee of Hotz. R. D. Kerley would go to work with Toshiba as a liaison who was tasked with finding other dealers in the country who wanted to sell. This was a great acquisition for Toshiba, but it did not help us in finding a dealer. TBS' locations fell into a different category for us, and did not have the same value for us in the field. Toshiba acquiring a dealer of this size made it virtually impossible for us to find a dealer in the market unless the TBS location consistently missed their sales targets.

My next hire was another valuable learning experience for me the hard way. I hired someone who might be considered a retread or old school DSM. He had been a DSM with Sharp in the past and I figured that my first experience with someone from the Sharp copier world had been great, why not add another. Boy was I wrong! The new person will just call him, Brett had a very boisterous personality. He was an extremely outgoing person and seemed to like everyone. However, he was a little touchy. At first, it did not seem to be a big problem. I got a few dealers saying that they did not want him in their dealership anymore. I started to do some research to see what the issue was with him and the dealers. It turns out that I found a couple of examples of him being too friendly with female salespeople from a specific dealership. I reported it to our human resources department and was told that the proper step would be to counsel him and tell him that if this occurred again, we would have to terminate him. You have heard the saying that a leopard does not change his spots. Well, that was true in this case and I terminated Brett. He had been a diligent worker, but just too friendly in an unwanted way. What I learned from this was to hire based on whether I thought a person would fit well in the role of a DSM at Toshiba, and not on what successes that person had in the past. This decision led me to one of my future hires who is still at Toshiba to this day.

After the experience with Brett, I decided that I would go back to my original strategy of hiring and add only people who had been selling directly to end user customers instead of an old school DSM from another company. This led me to hire Scott Frei. He would be the youngest member of my team for several years, but he was an adaptive learner and always looking to get better at supporting his dealers. Scott had sold Minolta copiers as a street representative in Indiana, so he was a natural fit for the territory that had come open because of my termination of the previous DSM. He had worked for another manufacturer for a brief period, but I later found out he did not like the experience. He was inclined to not want to work for another manufacturer. Fate intervened on this hire. Scott's brother worked for a Toshiba dealer called Bishop Business Equipment in Omaha. His brother's dealership was supported by one of my current DSM's. Todd Lee was the DSM in Omaha. He had been one of the keys to Bishop Business Equipment coming on board as a Toshiba dealer the year before I took over that state from the Central region. Bishops was a second-generation dealer. The company had been started by Dave Bishop's father in 1954. Since they became a Toshiba dealer in 1989, they have been consistently one of Toshiba Top dealers. They won one of our Toshiba dealer trips which was in 2018. We went to Vietnam and Cambodia that year. I did not know at the time that this would be my last Toshiba dealer trip. It was a truly memorable trip, something I would never have done on my own. Todd Lee encouraged Scott Frei. to meet with me about the open DSM position in Indiana. We had set up a meeting in Indianapolis at the airport. The meeting went very well, and Scott told his wife that he was going to take the job with Toshiba as one of my District Sales Managers. This was in 2002. Scott is still with Toshiba as of 2024 and was just recently promoted to a regional position. This hire showed me that having a good reputation in the industry was critical when hiring salespeople and collaborating with dealers. I learned over the years at Toshiba that the most important thing that you have in my role was a great reputation. The copier industry is very close-knit and dealers across the country talk about the support they are receiving from their manufacturer. If you had a reputation of being difficult to work with, or known as being less than a straight shooter, you are not going to get good dealers. In authoring this book, Scott gave me some interesting feedback. He told me a story of how my decision to hire him affected his life. Scott was successful at Toshiba and based on his success he and his family were able to buy their dream home in the country. Scott's new house was an old, converted farm, and his closest neighbor was about half a city block away. He was working from home one day and he saw smoke and fire coming out of the neighbor's house. Scott rushed over to the neighbors to see if he could help. He found the owner of the house was alone just sitting in the house in a state of shock. Fortunately, no one else was home except for the one man. He did not seem to realize that if he did not get out of the house, he could die from the fire. Scott tried to talk him into moving but it did not seem to register. Scott eventually virtually carried his neighbor to safety. He saved his neighbor's life that day. He said that if I had not made the decision to hire him, he could not have afforded to buy their dream home. And he would not have been there to save his neighbor. Sometimes you do not realize how the decision that you make can impact people that you never even met. Taking it a step further, if Todd had not said good things about me, Scott probably would not have taken the job, and he would not have been there to save his neighbor's life.

My role as a Regional Sales Manager changed over the years and I became a Regional Director. This did not mean more money, just more responsibility. It also meant more people reporting to me. This included software engineers, print management managers, and GEM (Government, Education, and Major Account Managers). There were also additional District Sales Managers. The number one responsibility for an RSM and later as a Regional Director was to make sure that the region hit our sales quota. This required constant contact with our dealers to ensure we were getting what production we need from their dealerships. It was a delicate balance of helping them grow with our team and developing other potential dealers in underproducing markets. This is when I discovered that my decisions could impact far more than my own team. The first step was to have all the right team members in place. I had now done that and now could focus on adding dealers where we needed them. Growing the dealers who had long term Toshiba potential. And getting rid of the dealers that were not going to be good Toshiba partner's long term. I now had to look at not only how my decisions could impact my team, but also the dealer owners and their employees that I might add or delete from a market. I took changes to our territory very seriously, and in most cases I made the right decision on who to recruit and who to cancel. The dealer's reactions to some of these decisions were sometimes very different than what I had anticipated.

Chapter 28
Let's Get Digital

Now that Toshiba was now a part of the digital world, it was critical that the sales team in the region have system engineers to assist our dealers with connecting our product to their networks. In most cases, the products connected easily, but because there were so many diverse types of networks direct support was critical for difficult installations. The systems engineers also help with pre-installation so that things would go seamlessly. Each region had two engineers. I inherited an engineer named Steve Smith from the color support team but had to add another one. Steve was one of the smartest people I have ever met in my life. In fact, he was so smart that sometimes the rest of the Midwest team could not understand what he was explaining to us. Since I had never hired an engineer, I asked Steve to assist me with the interviews. We interviewed several people for the job and found two whom we felt were the best qualified for the position. I decided that since both were equally qualified that I would go with the one that I felt had the most experience. Steve agreed with me, and we hired John Sidler. John started off great and seemed to be a perfect fit for our team.

About a month after he started, he then told me that he had to take a day off for a doctor's appointment. I told him that it was no problem, go to your appointment. The next day, I got a call from him to let me know that he had to take the rest of the week off. He told me that he had to go to the hospital for some additional tests, and that he would be out for at least another day or two. I got back with him at the end of the week to see how he was doing. He told me that they had found that he had a type of cancer and that was terminal. I was completely shocked. I told him I would reach out to the human resources department to find out what we should do. They told me that we should put John Sidler on medical leave, and that they would take care of the details. They then told me that John Sidler would not be coming back and that I was given the OK to hire a replacement person for the same role as a systems engineer. Since I had just interviewed people for this position when we hired John Sidler. I decided to reach out to the other qualified candidate to see if he was interested in the position. Ironically, he was also named John. John Moles told me that he was interested, and I told him what had happened. He understood, and I quickly hired John Moles for the position. John had run a small IT company that did network connectivity on Xerox products, so I was confident that he could smoothly transition to Toshiba.

Later, we learned that John S. had passed away. It was less than six months after he started with Toshiba. I was amazed at how quickly he had died. Shortly after his passing, his wife came into our Chicago office to return his Toshiba laptop and set up a time for us to pick up his Toshiba copier from their home. She thanked me for being so considerate about what had happened to her husband. And thanked me for how Toshiba had kept John on as an employee so that he would be covered fully be insurance until his passing. I was immensely proud of what Toshiba had done and made sure that all my team knew what type of company they worked for with Toshiba. John Moles has now been with Toshiba for over 25 years. He has held numerous roles and reported to different managers throughout his career at Toshiba, but He was the perfect hire for us in the Midwest. Not only was he a great engineer, but he also taught myself, and my team, more about connectivity with our products. He also was the one person who could translate what Steve S. was saying to a level that a non-IT person could understand. This was at a time when digital connectivity was still relatively new and having these two engineers on our team gave us a tremendous advantage when we were compared with some of the support systems in place of other manufacturers. Our dealers always thought we did a better job of supporting them when they sold products. Both of my system engineers were successful even if they were dramatically different in personalities.

Chapter 29
Is That Legal

In 1996 we had two dealers who covered parts of the Dayton, Ohio market. Neither of them was attaining their respective quotas. I went out to visit them both shortly after I became the RSM. I will not mention the dealerships' names to avoid embarrassing them and to avoid possible lawsuits. It was an interesting couple of visits. The smaller of the two dealerships was getting ready to sell their dealership to a non-Toshiba dealer in the market. I reminded them that they needed to give Toshiba thirty days' notice of such a change, and that we would then advise them if we were going to transfer the ability to sell Toshiba to the new owners. In this case since the Toshiba team was going to join the new dealership, I thought it would be home run. I thought having access to a larger dealer would help us in the market. However, just the opposite occurred. The new owners got rid of the people who had been selling Toshiba shortly after buying the company. They then started to convert the Toshiba machine base to Ricoh products. This facilitated another visit to Dayton.

I met with the new owners and advised them that if they did not increase their Toshiba numbers to at least the level of the previous dealership that I would have to take corrective action up to cancellation. I gave them 90 days to turn the numbers around and assigned them a growth target. They failed miserably, and did not attain even 50% of the target which was far less than assigned their quota. I knew then that they had no intention of selling Toshiba products long term. I advised the owner of the company, who happened to be a woman that I intended to cancel them. I informed her that they would receive written notice from us shortly that would inform them of the date of cancellation in writing. She was not happy about the decision on my part. She urged me to reconsider and told me that they would grow the Toshiba business but needed more time. I reminded her that we had already gone that route and that they had not attained the agreed targets. I left the office thinking that they understood what was going to happen and that they would simply continue to sell the Ricoh products that they had been switching to anyway. Transferring the agreement to the new dealers had been an unwise decision on my part. I vowed to be more diligent if the same sort of situation arose in the future.

I received a call the next week from our corporate attorney advising me that they had received a letter from the dealer in question stating that I and Toshiba were being sued for sexual discrimination by S. the owner. I was then advised by our attorney that I would be receiving a call to do a deposition. The deposition was done over the phone and recorded. I was asked if I cancelled the dealership in question because they were owned by a woman, and I replied, "I cancelled them because they were not selling our products and that they had been given written warning with a target for them to attain in 90-days, and they hit less than 50% of the target." All of which was done in accordance with the Toshiba agreement that they had accepted. This seemed to make the attorney happy, and the cancellation went through with no problem, and I never heard from that dealership again. My impression was that Toshiba told her that this was a frivolous lawsuit, and if they continued to pursue it, Toshiba would countersue. This reminded me to always document what you tell a dealer, especially if it is unwelcome news. I used this as a case in point to my team to always document every visit to a dealer so there is no question about when you were at their office, and what you covered with the sales team or ownership.

I am sure at this point you want to know what happened to the second dealer. We were fortunate with that dealership. It was owned by a man named Bob Von Derau. Bob was a former army ranger, so he and I got along well. He had decided that he no longer wanted to be in the copier business and had decided to sell his dealership. In his case, he was selling to a friend of his who already had offices in Cincinnati and Columbus. Dayton would be a perfect addition to his dealership. He was acquired by a man named Jim Donnellon. At that time Jim owned a company called ABS Business Products. Their main product line was Toshiba, and this was Jim's first acquisition. Jim Donnellon (below) had formerly been a DSM for Fujitsu facsimile products and decided that he wanted to become the owner of his own copier dealership. He started out partnering with two other men to form ABS Business Products. He eventually bought out the other two partners. And with Toshiba's help initially he continued to grow the business. ABS Products went on to be one of Toshiba's Dealer of the year and won several Toshiba trips. Jim indicated that one of the most memorable trips that we were on together was our trip to Scotland. Jim had some Scottish ancestry, so this trip was incredibly special to him. ABS had tremendous success in major accounts with the help of Toshiba, and this helped them to a point where Jim was able to buy a company named Donnellon McCarthy. Jim's brother owned this company. ABS continued to grow through both organic growth and acquisitions. By 2017 Jim had grown his business, now called Donnellon McCarthy Enterprises (DME) to over twenty-five million dollars. He also had acquired six additional companies that had offices in West Virginia, Illinois, Ohio, Indiana, and California.

Jim Donnellon & his wife on one of our dealer trips

Eventually we went from two dealers who were underperforming to one dealer who was over-performing and now that dealer covered three of our important markets in Southern Ohio for Toshiba. Our problem in Dayton had been resolved. It showed me that approaching people honestly and documenting everything was crucial when making any decision related to a dealer.

Chapter 30
Border Wars

There were many other markets that needed to be corrected in the Midwest. Some areas required adding new dealers while others needed the removal of dealers to grow the market. Two of the markets that needed correcting in the West Virginia/Kentucky area required a little bit of both. We had four dealers of note in those areas, and it was like Hatfield's and McCoy's. One of the dealers who was in the southern part of Kentucky had three key issues. First, his dealership was not hitting their quota. Second, he was selling outside of his territory and into another dealer's area. And third, he was passing off used equipment as newly refurbished. He was telling his customers that it was factory refurbished by Toshiba. Unfortunately, Toshiba did not have a refurbishing program, so this was clearly a misrepresentation to the customers. I met with the owner, who was a second generation, Toshiba dealer and told him that he had to stop selling out of his area, and that it was fraud to misrepresent product as factory remanufactured. I told him that he needed to start attaining his quota by selling within his own assigned territory and by abiding to the contract that they had signed. Less than thirty days later I received a call from one of his Toshiba customers. She told me that she was having problems with her copier and that Mr. K was not taking care of the issue and that since it was a factory refurbished unit, she wanted to return it to Toshiba. I asked her to tell me the serial number of the machine so that I could determine when the machine was made. I also asked her to tell me where her company was located. She told me that she worked for one of the local schools.

Just as I expected, Mr. K was up to his old tricks. The machine was over three years old and had not been sold to Mr. K. Additionally, the customer was not located in Mr. S's authorized territory. It had been sold to another dealer in another region and was a lease return from another dealer. I contacted the other dealer just to confirm that they had not sold it to Mr. K's dealership. They had not, in fact they told me the end user that they had leased the copier to three years earlier. I now had all the information that I needed to confront Mr. K with this latest violation and told him that he was in violation of his contract, and that I would send him a termination letter. He of course threatened to sue Toshiba. I told him to go ahead and once it went to court and they found out what he had been doing he would probably end up in jail. He decided not to sue. He ended up taking on another product line. They seemed to be a lot more laxed than Toshiba as far as how they represent themselves to the public. You might ask what happened to a poor end user customer who had the old, refurbished machine? We shipped an updated version of the machine to the dealer who was authorized in the territory and told him to install it and that he could keep the old machine for parts. The customer was delighted and thanked me for the new unit. She also wrote me a note about a month later telling me how happy she was with the other dealer. This dealership was also located in Southern Kentucky and was one of our most loyal dealers. Ironically, fixing the customers problem took care of her issue and solved the territory issue. He had been a Toshiba dealership for over twenty-five years at the time, and he was ecstatic that he would no longer have to listen to complaints from customers and Mr. K's dealership encroaching on his territory. The decision to make this change was a home run for Toshiba's reputation in the area. The customer who wrote me the letter also gave me a few leads over the years which I was able to give to the proper dealership. She also eventually changed to another school district and because of her positive experience with Toshiba, she got that district to buy Toshiba copiers for their district.

Speaking of Hatfield's and Mc Coy's, I had a different type of problem on the West Virginia, Kentucky border. The situation involved two of our smaller dealers. Sometime before I was with Toshiba the two states were in different regions. One of the dealerships was named Aaron's. They had initially been part of the eastern region, and the other dealer named Van Dyke's had been set up by the Midwest region. Unfortunately, when Aaron's was in the eastern region they had been given some counties in Kentucky, and the dealer from the Midwest was given a couple of counties in West Virginia. As it ended up the two dealers had six counties that were covered by both dealerships. Since the area does not really have any major markets that dealers would constantly end up calling on the same accounts. This caused issued for the customer as to whom they should buy from, since both dealers would represent themselves as the better choice. It also made Toshiba look bad because we could not represent Toshiba at bids with either dealership. We did not want it to appear that we favored one dealer over the other.

It appeared that my predecessors either did not know about the issue or thought that the dealers should just fight it out. I decided that since both dealers were good Toshiba dealers it would be much better to solve the problem permanently. My goal was to try and make both dealers happy. I reached out to both dealers in 1998 and told them I would like to have a conference call with both dealerships, and that I had a solution that I wanted to run past them. Once I got both dealers on the phone, I told them I would like each of them to give up some counties. They initially went crazy. I let them rant for a minute and then said let me roll out my proposal. Aarons would give up four counties located in Kentucky on the border, and Van Dyke's would give up two counties located in West Virginia. I also checked the business density for the four counties on one side versus the two counties on the other side and told them they were virtually the same. I had also told them that because the business density was similar for the counties, it would have negligible impact on their dealership's quota, and they would both have clean markets assuming they continued to hit their quota's. They both laughed and thought about it for a minute and agreed to my solution. Solomon would have been proud of me on this one. I told both dealers that I would have a letter sent out to them with the revised counties I had recommended.

Since both dealerships had been so cooperative, I told them I would set up to visit them and thank them for their assistance. I scheduled two separate visits with them. The first visit worked out well with Van Dykes. The son of Gary Van Dyke was getting married soon and my wife and I were invited to the festivities by Gary. So, I was able to tie my visit to their son's pending nuptials. The second meeting would be at Aaron's. Aaron's dealership is in Huntington, West Virgina. Huntington is the home of Marshall University. In 1970, Marshall University lost their football team in a plane crash near the Tri-State Airport that killed seventy-five members of the football team and coaches. This airport is on top of a mountain. I had rented cars several times after arriving at the airport and was amazed at the long winding road to get down from the airport. I had flown into Tri-State Airport more than once with no issues, but this time was different. On our approach to landing at the airport we touched down and then went back up into the air. We did not know what had happened at the time. The pilot came on the intercom and told us that as he was landing a truck had started across the runway and he had to abort the landing as to avoid hitting the truck. Once I got off the plane, I thought about how my decision to set up this visit might have led to the end of my life. It was a sobering thought! I considered myself incredibly lucky at the time that nothing bad had happened to our plane.

Chapter 31
On Wisconsin!

Over the years, as both a DSM and an RSM, I had to try to recruit dealers in areas of need. Sometimes it is a slow process to find the right dealership, and to get them to believe that adding Toshiba or changing to Toshiba is of benefit to them. The key is to be persistent. The more times you contact a dealership over the years the more comfortable they are that you are going to be around and that making a change might be an innovative idea.

When I was DSM, I had the state of Wisconsin added to my territory for about a year. Once I got to Wisconsin, I looked at our coverage and saw that we were in decent shape in the greater Milwaukee market and in good shape in the greater Madison market, but the rest of the state was a mess. Adding a dealer in Wisconsin is overly complicated because of their franchise laws which do not allow you to cancel the dealers that are currently in the market selling your products. This means you must be careful in how you proceed either by adding a dealer or figuring out how to eliminate a dealer. In a perfect world you would simply grow the dealers that you have, but this is not a perfect world. My first visit was to our dealer in Appleton, their name was ABM. They were a smaller Toshiba dealer, but they covered both Appleton and Green Bay markets. They had been in the office equipment business since the days of mechanical typewriters. The owner Bill Mauer was an older gentleman at the time I visited, and his plan was to hand the business off to his son who already worked at the dealership. They were doing a respectable job and then Bill decided to retire and put his son in charge. Once his son got control of the business, he found out that overseeing a dealership was challenging work. He was approached by the Canon dealer called MBM, who wanted to acquire them. MBM was the smallest of the three Canon dealers who between them covered the entire state of Wisconsin. ABM sold to MBM. The owners of MBM did everything correctly in acquiring one of our Toshiba dealers, so we approved the transfer of the Toshiba agreement to them since we had no other coverage in the area. As soon as we gave them approval to sell Toshiba, they started to flip the base. Being new with Toshiba at the time, I was appalled that they would outright lie to me about their plan. I should have known better. A learned a valuable lesson to never assume that a dealer is telling you their entire plan.

The situation in Appleton and Green Bay was unacceptable and in Wisconsin, you cannot cancel a dealer because they are protected by franchise laws. I met with them a few months into our relationship and confronted them about what they were doing. I then asked them to resign and told them I was going to expand our dealer from Sheboygan into that market, and they would be much better off pushing their Canon line than trying to explain why Toshiba had added a second dealer to the market. Shockingly, they agreed and sent me a letter resigning as a Toshiba dealer. Little did I know what the underlying reason was as to why they resigned so easily. Less than a year later MBM sold to one of the larger Canon dealers who cover both Madison and Milwaukee at the time. I assumed that having only one product line that matched the other dealers made them more inviting to be acquired.

Now that MBM had agreed to resign, I immediately met with Dick Holstein. Dick owned a small Toshiba dealer in Sheboygan and Oshkosh markets. He had bought out the previous owner named Robert Ross who had started the business in 1961. I thought that Ross Office Machines could give us the coverage we needed in Appleton and Green Bay. I told them they would be the only dealer in that market if they hit our agreed target for the market. My plan worked for the second time, and Ross Office Machines (later Ross Imaging) now had Appleton and Green Bay as a part of their territory, but it had taken over a year to fix that market. A few years later, Dick decided to retire and sold the Ross Office Machines to Tom S in 2003. Tom had been Dick's top salesperson over the years, but he was not very skilled at running a business. He was extremely hard on his sales team and could not keep salespeople, which cause the sales to plummet. He realized that the business was not growing and that his best move would be to sell the business to someone else. In 2005, Tom S. sold the business to another Toshiba dealer named Imagetec. Ross Office had won several bands on the State of Wisconsin copier contract with Toshiba, so there was a revenue stream that the new owner did not want to lose. The Wisconsin copier contract was quite simple. There were six bands in the contract based on copier speeds and set accessories. There were two copiers that won in each band. All state entities needed to buy off that contract. We ended up with a stronger dealer covering all three of the secondary markets of Appleton, Green Bay, and Sheboygan, better than we had ever had in the past. However, the story does not end with Imagetec buying Ross Office Machines, now renamed Ross Imaging, but more on that later.

I did not have any great prospects in the outlying markets so I decided to see if I could improve what we had in Milwaukee and then Madison. In Milwaukee we had a long time Toshiba dealer, called James Office Equipment. They had not really grown significantly in the four years I had been with Toshiba at the time. Now that I was the RSM, I wanted to sit down with him and figure out what we could do to help them grow in the future with us. I had also been prospecting in the market and had not found anyone that we could bring on as a dealer that would give us what we needed. We had another small dealer owned by Stan Cozzuli, but he had just sold his business to one of his employees and I decided to not transfer the Toshiba contract to the new people. This allowed us the opportunity to add another dealer without increasing the number of dealers we had in the market. James Office Equipment was now our only dealer in the greater Milwaukee market, and they were dual line dealers at the time. Their other product line was Mita/Kyocera.

I set up a meeting with both Lola and Tom Tegeder, who owned the company. Lola was the owner, but Tom oversaw running the company to see what we might be able to do to help them. At the time they were operating out of a small building that looked like it had been a Mexican restaurant in its former life. Lola came into the meeting first; Tom had a habit of always being the last one in the meetings. She decided to show me some pictures of when her husband and her had started the business. She indicated that they had started the business in 1977. Lola worked in the office and did all the books, and her husband was responsible for sales and his brother helped with servicing their customers' equipment. They had started fixing copiers out of a room in their home and stayed that way until they started to fill up their basement with old copiers. At that point they moved to their first office building. Shortly after they moved to the building they were in when we first met, Lola's husband passed away unexpectedly in 1984. Tom's uncle was also involved with the management of the company. Unfortunately, he also died shortly after Tom's father. So, the job of operating the company fell to Lola and to Tom. This was in the early nineties. Tom was in his early twenties at the time and very new to the business of running a company. The good news was that he was incredibly open to any suggestions that would help him grow their business. I met with Lola and Tom in 1994 and told both that there was no way based on their size and their location in a major market that they could satisfy two manufacturers. based on their current size. I asked them if they had to pick one manufacturer which one they would prefer. They told me the Toshiba products had been more dependable in the field, but the Mita products were less expensive. I saw the opportunity that I needed to get them to go single line with Toshiba. I told them if I could put together a program to give them pricing that was equal to or better than Mita and give them a rebate for dropping Mita to help defer the cost of going single line would they be interested? They said they would be interested if we gave them a program in writing that laid out what we would do for them. I told them that I need to know what their current monthly sales for both product lines were over the last two years. I also asked them what percentage of growth they were targeting for growth over the next two years. They looked as if they had not really set a finite target for two years. They furnished me with the information I needed to build a plan and make a proposal to the VP of Sales for Toshiba on what I wanted to do. The dealer development plan I laid out for them targeted 10% annual growth over the next three years and included a bonus for furnishing me a letter stating that they were resigning as Mita dealer within the first year of the program. I also add a small bonus for them for adding manpower which would help them grow the business. This part of the package for manpower gave them a rebate for each salesperson they added after the completion of one year of sales with their company. Toshiba approved my plan even though they were not sure that the dealer would hit all the targets. I presented the plan to Tom and Lola, and they signed off on it. It took them almost a month to return the signed document. I learned that Tom did not move very quickly when making decisions he liked to get input from several sources first. I think at the time he was a little apprehensive about committing to something over a three-year period, but I have a feeling that Lola told him it was good for both sides and that they should take the deal. Over the next fifteen years, Tom and I worked closely on innovative ideas to help them grow their business with Toshiba. Eventually, through a series of twists and turns, James Office Equipment helps Toshiba out in other markets. Eventually, they changed their name to James Imaging Systems and continued to focus on growing their business through organic growth of their customer base and through acquisitions. The first Toshiba dealer they acquired was a small Toshiba dealer who was in the northern counties of their territory. The dealership was named Marnett's Office Solutions. It was owned by a man named Lee Marnett. Lee was a holocaust survivor and his approach to business was very different. Marnett's was a small dealership with just Lee and one salesperson. It was a terrific addition for James Office Equipment to get started with in the acquisitions business. Their next Toshiba acquisition was Ross Imaging from Imagetec. They also added some print management companies to diversify what they were offering to their customers. They were named Toshiba's dealer of the year in 2017. They also won several other Toshiba dealer trips. They have continued to grow their business today and are still a woman owned private company. At this point, I felt that Milwaukee was now in good hands. My decision to focus on growing James Office Equipment back in 1994 had been a great decision and ended up causing a chain of events that impacted several of my Wisconsin dealers over the years. James Imaging Systems, like several of the Midwest Toshiba dealers, won our dealer of the year award in 2017. I cannot imagine how many individuals were affected by the program I started with James Imaging in 1994. After about three years of solid production at Ross Imaging, Rich C. decided that it was time to sell that part of his company for a profit. He told me what he wanted to do, and I made Tom Tegeder aware of the fact that Imagetec wanted to sell Ross Imaging. Tom Tegeder of James Imaging and Rich Cucco of Imagetec did not have the best relationship at the time. However, something strange happened about the time Ross Imaging was up for sale. Toshiba had a shortage of toner due to a strike at the port of Los Angeles. Imagetec reached out to James Imaging to see if they could buy some toner from them. This started the two of them talking and the rest is history. I cannot say that letting Tom know about what Rich wanted to do cause the sale to occur or that I had caused the toner shortage, but sometimes things just fall into place. However, in the dealer world money is king. After a couple of months of negotiation, the deal was closed, and Ross Imaging was now a part of James Imaging. We now had the best coverage we could have asked for, covering the eastern half of the state of Wisconsin. I never would have thought that when I had that first meeting with James Imaging twenty years earlier that they would end up buying a dealership from one of their archrival dealers.

Chapter 32
Persistence Pays

I also reached out to another Canon dealer on the other side of the state. The dealership was called E O Johnson. At the time I started calling on them E O was still active in the company. I made it a point to call him every three months like clockwork. After a while E O would laugh and tease me about being late for the quarterly call. On the fifth quarterly call, E O told me that he would like to meet with me. I said it was no problem and quickly set up a visit. I met with him and his upper management team, and pitched why they might want to add Toshiba to their product mix. They were polite and told me that they were happy with Canon and Ricoh and did not plan to add another line, but they would contact us if something changed. I had recently been promoted to RSM and gained Minnesota, South Dakota, and North Dakota to the Midwest region. I also gained Todd Lee as a DSM. I told Todd that I wanted him to reach out to E O Johnson every quarter just as I had been. The good news is we now had something additional to offer that they might be interested in. We could now offer them the ability to sell Toshiba in Minneapolis. At the time, we had a Toshiba branch in Minneapolis but no dealer. The branch locations were called Toshiba Business Solutions, in this case Minneapolis (TBS-MN). Toshiba Corporate was OK with us adding a dealer to the market because the branch was underperforming at the time. Todd reached out to E O Johnson, just as I had and when we mentioned Minneapolis, they had some interest. They had also been in negotiations with our small Toshiba dealer called Computer Business Solutions in Eau Claire, Wisconsin. The dealer owner there was a man named Ed Nakla. Ed happened to have been born in Egypt. I had never had a dealer from that country and found it interesting. Ed's background was with computers, and he felt that this was where his future in business lay. He indicated that he was negotiating with E O Johnson to sell the copier part of the business. I told him that I would approve transferring his dealer agreement to them if they intended to become a Toshiba dealer. I am not sure if that was the catalyst that made them bring on Toshiba, but I am sure it was a part of their decision to partner with us.

We set up another meeting with E O Johnson after the pending acquisition. The timing was interesting because E O was retiring from the company, and his daughter Mary Jo Johnson would be the new owner with Roger King as the new president. Roger was a great person to work with. He was extremely helpful with the addition of Toshiba to their product offerings. And we convinced him that Toshiba would be a terrific addition for them in Minneapolis and help them in other markets. Roger knew that Ricoh and Canon were not going to set them up in Minneapolis because each of them already had strong dealers in that market and did not want to rock the boat with someone from outside of the Minneapolis market. It took us eight years to get E O Johnson on board, but we did it. We ran into one unusual problem in adding E O Johnson to our dealer network. The problem was a small dealer in La Crosse, who carried both Toshiba and Canon. He was doing little with Toshiba and did not think we could find anyone better in the market. Every time we reach out to a small potential dealer in the market, they end up either retiring or selling their small dealership to someone else in the market. The owner of the dealer in La Crosse was right, until we convinced E O Johnson to come on board as a Toshiba dealer. He then reacted in a way that I had never expected. He took Toshiba and E O Johnson to court for restraint of trade. The DSM at time had changed with Todd Lee who had moved on to the TBS-MN position.

The new DSM was someone who had transferred from a GEM role at Toshiba to a DSM role. His name was John Swisher. John had been a DSM for Canon for several years and felt that the DSM position aligned with his skill set better than the GEM role. Ironically, John Swisher had been the DSM who supported E O Johnson with Canon, so they were incredibly happy to have him again. John and I had no idea what would happen next after the strange dealer reaction to our adding E O Johnson.

Chapter 33
The Court's in Session

Shortly after bringing on E O Johnson, John and I were contacted by our corporate office. We were told that we would have to testify in court and show why our addition of E O Johnson to the dealer mix was justified. Toshiba and E O Johnson were being sued by the current Toshiba dealer in the market. He was claiming restraint of trade as his basis for the lawsuit. Our legal team immediately submitted a countersuit against the dealer in question. Toshiba got their suit submitted first so that it would stay in the state of Wisconsin courts and not Federal court. Once we got to court the strangest twist possible happened. The dealer owner from La Crosse got on the stand and presented his side of the story. John Swisher was set to give his testimony next, and then it would be my turn. The attorney for the dealer asked the judge for a fifteen-minute recess to discuss what they wanted to do next.

After the dealer owner and his attorney met, they felt that they were going to lose the case. The dealer owner and his attorney then presented Toshiba with a counter proposal. He agreed to drop his lawsuit and resign as a Toshiba dealer. Toshiba agreed to give him a small parting gift for his cooperation. John Swisher and I never had to testify. We were both shocked, as were our attorneys. I was now two for two in lawsuits from dealers.

Fortunately, I only had two cases of suits from dealers in my tenure with Toshiba. Again, it had paid off to have copious notes and a strong paper trail to show what we had done. E. O. Johnson is still a Toshiba dealer in good standing to this day.

They are a first-class dealer and a great partner with Toshiba, and we had plenty of opportunities to grow our business with them. In fact, in one of their first years with Toshiba they won our dealer trip, and we took our dealers to Italy that year. My wife and I attended several events with Mary Jo and her husband on the trip, and they seemed to be having a wonderful time. Hopefully, my successors can reap the benefit of the groundwork that I laid. It took our team starting with me as a DSM over eight years and numerous visits to get E O Johnson on board as a Toshiba dealer, but since they were by far the best dealer in the Western part of Wisconsin it was worth the effort. In this case our years of persistence paid off, but we still had other markets that needed to be fixed.

Chapter 34
Knowledge Is Power

The last market we had to address in Wisconsin was Madison. Our current dealer in Madison was G.I. Office Technology, formerly G.I. Office Solutions. When I started with Toshiba, GI Office Solutions was a single line Minolta dealer. I first met them in my first six months with Toshiba. We had started carrying facsimile products and they were considering adding fax to the products they sold. This was in 1990, and Minolta did not have much to offer regarding facsimile products.

At the time Wisconsin was not my territory. I was asked to do the facsimile presentation by my boss because Barry did not know anything about our facsimile products. Barry was one of the old school DSMs who left Toshiba shortly after Dick Walker became president of Toshiba. I must have done a respectable job in the presentation because they came on board as a facsimile dealer at the time. We were allowed to set up facsimile-only dealers in markets where we had no copier representation. The hope was that they would like our fax products and the support we gave them so much that they would decide to add our copiers to their product line.

A few years later in 2003 everything changed for their dealership. Konica and Minolta had merged to form one company. However, as with all mergers one side is the dominant partner. In this case it was Konica which was not good for G.I. because Konica had a branch office in Madison. Greg Tipple, the owner, was sure that they would not get the same support that they had gotten from Minolta, and he decided to look at another product line. Since he already had the Toshiba facsimile line adding Toshiba copiers seemed like an easy addition. Knowing our facsimile products and bringing them on board as a fax only dealer had paid off. We jumped at the chance to add them to our copier dealers. They were the second largest dealer in the market at the time and very professional. Konica Minolta did not like them taking on another product line and asked them to resign after they began to sell Toshiba.

Since they did not feel they could support two lines they resigned. We now had a single line Toshiba dealer in Madison. They did very well with Toshiba for several years. Greg even won a couple of Toshiba trips. However, their sales team was still the same eight people they had when they became a Toshiba dealer so their sales could not keep pace with the growth we needed from that market. I knew I had to do something to supplement our sales in the greater Madison market. We need to have some insurance. We had been looking for better coverage in Madison since 2011.

After contacting all the main prospects in the market, I decided that I would try the startup type of dealer again. I contacted a small printer dealer in Kenosha in 2017 and talked to them about becoming a Toshiba dealer. They were small so I decided I would only give them a few counties at a time. I knew he wanted to go to Madison Wisconsin, and towards Rockford Illinois. I set him up with four counties to start with and told him once he hit the market target for those four counties I would expand him. I also gave him some funds to train his technicians. The good news was that it worked out exactly as I had wanted it to. He hit the market targets, and we added a few more counties without dramatically impacting on our dealers in Rockford or Madison. Hopefully, my instincts were right, and he would continue to grow after my retirement.

Chapter 35
Branch vs. Dealership

During the quest to fix all the holes in the Wisconsin market there were dozens of visits to dealers who had no interest in adding another product line or completely dropping the line had currently. Others had interest but either wanted more than we wanted to give them regarding territory, or they could not generate the dollars we needed from the market in question. Adding to the issue of adding dealers was the beginning of large dealers buying smaller dealers to become mega dealers, and manufacturers buying dealers to add to their branches. It was like playing a giant chess game, except in this case all the chess pieces were actual people. At the time, when I had to make the decision on whom to add or not add, I did not really give much thought as to how it might impact the prospect dealer if we did not move forward. I always thought about how our dealers would be impacted but not the other side.

While we were adding dealers in markets where we had underproduction, Toshiba, like other manufacturers, had joined the fray of adding to their branches. In some cases, these dealers that Toshiba purchased helped us like the Toshiba Business Solutions-Minneapolis acquisition helped us, but there were other cases where it hurt our recruiting of new dealers. Dealers did not want to compete against branches. They always felt that the branch would get preferential treatment. Ironically, in Toshiba case we usually bent over backwards to make sure the playing field was level. In fact, we often gave the dealer preference, but perception is reality to the dealer. One of these cases where it had hurt us was in North Dakota. Toshiba bought a non-Toshiba dealer who also sold other items besides copiers. This purchase alienated the small Toshiba dealer we had in North Dakota, and he decided to change product lines immediately. Not only did he change lines, but he took on the Lanier product line. This happens to be the same line as the dealer Toshiba had acquired and made a part of TBS-MN.

This decision turned out to be a huge mistake for all of us. The dealer Toshiba acquired sold more Musak type of product than they did copiers. In fact, over half of their sales were tied to non-copier products. This coupled to the fact that our now ex-Toshiba dealer was going after the base of copiers that he had sold to Toshiba, greatly reduced the value of what Toshiba had acquired. Additionally, the location was far too distant from our Minneapolis location to be supported correctly. I am confident that in retrospect Toshiba would probably not have acquired this dealer. Eventually, Toshiba ended up selling this Toshiba location to our dealer in South Dakota for an extremely low price. The bigger problem it created was that we would have little to no representation in North Dakota for some time. Not having a dealer in this market was entirely unacceptable for Toshiba, because Toshiba had a toner plant in Mitchell, South Dakota that made all the toner for the United States for Toshiba copier products.

In the meantime, we had been prospecting in the western part of South and North Dakota to try and find someone who could give us better coverage. These markets are unique because there is an extremely low population density, and it is over a large area. As we prospected for a dealer, we found that there were only three dealers in the two states that could give us adequate coverage. One of them was a large Canon dealer, called Best Business. The owner was a lady named Betty Best, and she had no desire to talk to us about another line. The second one was a Kyocera dealer called Century Business. The third one was the most interesting for us. It was a company called A & B Business Systems. A & B Business was a company that started business in 1981. It was founded by Art Sinkey and Bill Kominga thus the name A & B.

After many years Dennis Aanenson purchased the company in 1993. Since there were so few good options for copier dealerships in South Dakota in the nineties, Ricoh allowed A & B to carry multiple Ricoh labels. In their case, they carried both the Ricoh and the Savin brand. Both brands were the exact same product. In fact, when the dealer ordered these products, they came with stickers that could be placed on the unit for any of the brands they were authorized to sell. This was a wonderful way for Ricoh to have coverage throughout the state for major accounts regardless of which brand the customers' corporate location was purchasing. Initially, we got A & B to come on as a Toshiba dealer as a third line in part of the area we needed coverage. Once we got them on board, I decided to be creative. We had to have coverage for seventy plus major account units we had in the field, and things were getting desperate after TBS-MN had bought the only Toshiba dealer we had in North Dakota. All we had left was an exceedingly small Toshiba dealer in Mitchell, South Dakota and they could not possibly cover the major accounts or grow as much as we need. I told my DSM to set up a meeting with the owner of A & B, Dennis Aanenson.

Dennis was by far the most interesting dealer I had ever worked with. Since the potential customer population was so limited in South and North Dakota with a total population of both states of less than 1.8 million people. To put that into perspective that is about half the population of Chicago. Dennis took on a different approach to the limited potential in the market. He decided to sell many items that were not part of the normal copier distribution channel. Dennis had a wine distribution company. He also had a coffee distributorship. He had a grocery store with a deli program. He owned a truck wash for over the road trucks. He then sold the dirt that was washed off the trucks to local farmers for fertilizer. And lastly, he had his own line of beef jerky.

I decided that we would target A & B for expansion, due to Dennis's desire to think outside of the box. I decided to make him an offer that he could not refuse. I learned this from my Italian grandfather, Rocco Marchese. I met with Dennis Aanenson, the owner, and asked him how much he thought it would cost to take on a much larger territory and cover all North and South Dakota for us. Dennis initially laughed at me and told me that Toshiba could not afford it. I told him to humor me and tell me a number that would work for him. He told me that it would cost him hundreds of thousands of dollars to expand with a newer product line. I asked him if he needed the money all at once. He looked shocked and told me that it would be something they would need gradually. I told him that I knew what he needed and if I could get him what he needed or more would he take on the extra territory we discussed? He told me yes, but the program would have to be in writing. We set up a follow-up meeting for the next week.

Once I left Dennis's office, I immediately reached out to the VP of Sales and told him I had a plan to not only give us coverage for all our major accounts in North and South Dakota, but to also give us a way into helping A & B become the largest dealer in the market. He asked me to lay out the plan. Here is a basic overview of how the plan would work on the five-year plan.

1. A & B would immediately take over the seventy major account machines in the area and receive the revenue stream for these products. This was several thousand dollars a month.

2. Toshiba would ship any required parts to bring the major account machines up to original performance at no charge. This would ensure a profit on those accounts for A & B.

3. Toshiba would issue a credit for each fiscal half for the next five years. Ten credits totaling several thousand dollars.

4. Toshiba would issue an additional credit for adding a sales/service location in Rapid City. This would give us better coverage in North Dakota.

The total value of all credits would be more than the figure that Dennis said he needed over the first five years.

I then went back to A & B the next week with my proposal and Dennis signed the Dealer Development Funds Agreement (DDF). Creativity had paid off. We now have coverage in both North and South Dakota. This all started in 2000, and by 2005 A & B was one of the top ten dealers in the Midwest. A & B now covered more counties than any other dealer in the United States with counties in South Dakota, North Dakota, Montana, Iowa, Nebraska, Wyoming, and Minnesota. Over the five-year program A & B attained every target of the program I had put together and received all the funds in the plan.

In 2005 A & B won their first Toshiba trip. It was a trip to South Africa and Dennis sent his partner at the time Alan on that trip. I found out that Dennis did not like to travel overseas. A & B continued to grow in dollars with Toshiba every year and was still doing well in 2024. This was one of the most difficult and best dealer additions that I did while at Toshiba. I had made an excellent choice in how to cover these two difficult states. If I had not found a creative solution to add A & B, Toshiba would have been in trouble in the Dakotas. This showed that if you think creatively and make the right offer it will pay off eventually.

Hapkido Black Belt

Chapter 36
Midlife Crisis

In 2001, I turned fifty years old and had a midlife crisis. I decided that there were two things that I wanted to accomplish in life that I had always said I was going to do. The first was to start martial arts and the second was to learn to play the guitar. Since I was turning fifty, I thought it would be best to do martial arts first while I was still young. I began by trying to find out what discipline was right for me to pursue. We had several to choose from in my area. I plan to look at Taekwondo. Shotokan, and Hapkido. They seemed to be the most popular. I ruled out Taekwondo because I did not care for the studio. It seemed to be more generic. I ruled out Shotokan because it seemed geared to larger individuals and that was not me.

I then walked into a small studio and watched the Grand Master teaching class. He was a smaller Korean man, about my size only a little lighter. I knew immediately I was in the right place. Traditional Martial Arts, a form of Hapkido was going to be my choice. I waited for the class to finish and then started talking to Grand Master Chu Ma. I asked him if I could enroll, and he told me I could and that his classes for new students were a mix of children and adults. I signed up and got my first uniform and my white belt. I went religiously three times a week initially for the first five years. I worked my way up through all the color belts and the test to achieve each of them until I got my first- degree black belt at age fifty-five (above). I continued to pursue Traditional Martial Arts with Master Ma for another seven years.

I had worked my way up to a third-degree black belt and

was now an instructor. I loved teaching classes and watching the children as we helped them go from one belt to the next. Some of them eventually became black belts and helped teach classes to the newer kids. Unfortunately, at age 63, I had to stop taking classes. I had to have a knee replacement, and my doctor said I should probably not continue with the martial arts classes. In the meantime, I did take guitar lessons for a year and discovered that I had truly little talent for the guitar. My decision to take on Martial Arts helped keep me focused and sane through some of the hard years at Toshiba.

I also made it a point to get regular checkups with my doctor after what had happened with my father. At one of these checkups, my family doctor thought I should have a stress test. I am not sure why exactly, but he thought it was a suitable time to do one. He may have saved my life. As it turns out, they found out that I had an aneurysm just above my heart. Doctor Liesen told me that it was something that they would need to monitor but that was it for now. This discovery impacted my thinking dramatically for a while. I now knew that I could die if the aneurysm gave way. For several months I had a tough time coping with this newfound medical problem. Fortunately, between working and martial arts I kept busy and eventually got passed it. Little did I know what was in store for me in the future on the medical front.

Chapter 37
All That Glitters

Sometimes you must work hard to accomplish something. That was the usual case in recruiting dealers. On occasion something happens that seems to be too good to be true. Recruiting dealers was always something that we did. You never knew when one of your current dealers would sell to someone else or take on another product line. In Indianapolis we had a good dealer called HPS. HPS was owned by a dealer named Leon Mordoh (below). Leon was great guy. He had been in the copier business all his life in various positions. He was a short Jewish man who could charm anyone into doing what he wanted them to do. In 1991, Brian Kohn was the DSM for Indiana. He convinced HPS to come on board as a Toshiba dealer. They did an excellent job for us and won several trips. But like all things they end. Leon decided to sell his dealership to a friend of his, who happened to be a Toshiba dealer in Chicago. The dealer was Imagetec who was in the expansion mode at the time, and this would be their first acquisition. This acquisition by Imagetec took place in 2006. Imagetec did a fantastic job with Toshiba in growing the business for the next two years. Then in 2008 Imagetec sold their Indianapolis location to Toshiba. It became Toshiba Business Solutions-Indiana. This was good for Toshiba overall, but not so good for our dealer representation in that market.

Leon Mordoh (second left) in Scotland with Rich Cucco

We were now without a dealer in that market. Toshiba's philosophy on markets where we had a branch was to leave the market branch only, if the branch was hitting the market targets and to add a dealer the market needed to be subsidized. Indianapolis was one of those markets that needed a dealer to help hit the targets. We had worked on getting a quality dealer in that market for years but could not find the right fit. None of the larger dealers wanted to compete against a branch location. They all thought that the branch would always get better pricing. We could not find a prospect that fits the market for years, and we had basically reconciled ourselves to the fact that we would not find one. Then Scott Frei, the DSM for Indiana called me and told me that he had received a call from a company called Cannon IV, and that they wanted to talk to us. They were a Panasonic copier dealership at the time and Panasonic had told Cannon IV that they were going to discontinue selling copiers. We set up a meeting to discuss Toshiba with them. We wanted to get in to see them before anyone else did. This seemed like an excellent opportunity. The meeting was set for the next week. This was in the winter of 2012. Scott called me the day before and asked me if I was still coming because of the weather. I told him that I would be flying in and for him to pick me up at the airport. It was snowing in Chicago and by the time I got to Indianapolis it was a blizzard. Scott picked me up in his Buick sedan. I had hoped he would rent something that was a four-wheel drive, but this was his personal car. We started driving very slowly to their office. There was about eight inches of snow already on the ground. When we got close to their location the snow was even deeper and the street, they were on had not yet plowed. I said to myself, "what have I gotten myself into?" Their facilities were impressive. The owner started telling us about how they were one of HP's largest printer dealers in the US. They told us about all the accounts that they had and how they needed a full copier line to really maximize these accounts. In looked around and I did not see a copier showroom, which I thought was very strange, but since they had been told that Panasonic was done with that business I assumed that they had sold what they had so they could move on with a clean slate.

We did our presentation to them, and when we finished, they said they wanted to come on board with Toshiba. They asked us what paperwork they needed to fill out and handed us copies of their financials at the meeting. Scott gave them the documents that they needed to complete and said he would pick them up next week since he lived in an Indianapolis suburb. They told us Scott could pick them up tomorrow and wanted to know when they could start selling Toshiba products. We told them we could fast track the paperwork, and have it done in two weeks, and that we would have our service manager come out so he could get them set up for training. Scott and I left and we high fived on how easily this had gone. Big mistake on our part. We got all the paperwork done and got them on board, but from that point on it was like pulling teeth to get them to do what they needed to do. They did not want to go to service training on all the products. This is only a three-week process so it should not have been an issue. We told them we needed them to bring in demo inventory so we could train their sales staff. They did not want to bring in any products unless they had them sold. They said they would sell them from brochures. We knew this did not work and finally got them to bring in one machine so that Scott could work with the salespeople on training. Scott set up training and came in to do it, and the machine was not there, they had sold it. Life with Cannon IV continued like that for years. Eventually, they sold their company to a mega dealer on the east coast, and we thought that our frustration with them was over since the company that bought them was an actual copier dealer. No such luck, the new owners were just as bad, except they were even slower to act. I learned from my decision that if something happens too easily, it probably is going to have issues later. Eventually, Scott and I found another dealer to bring on in the market in 2019 shortly before I retired. I hope they will do better for Scott and Toshiba than Cannon IV did, and that this new dealer can give them the production that they need out of the Indianapolis market.

Chapter 38
One for the Road

By 2017 we had decent coverage throughout the Midwest in all our key markets with one exception. The exception was the central part of Iowa with the center of the issue being Des Moines. Over the years we had tried several different solutions in the market. We started with a small single line dealer called Copy Systems, but they did not give us the coverage we needed. We then expanded our dealer from Omaha, Bishop Business Equipment into the Des Moines market and help subsidize them. Bishops had been tremendously successful for us in the Omaha market so expanding them seemed like a win-win situation. Unfortunately, the customers in the Iowa market gravitated to local dealers and Bishop's left the market after a couple of years. We had to find a fix for the Des Moines market. My DSM in the market was Kennedy Cross, and he continued to call on all the large dealers in the market repeatedly. We were not having much luck but then something changed at Toshiba.

Toshiba had partnered with Lexmark, so we decided to try a different tactic and approach the largest Lexmark distributor in the market. The company we targeted was called Access Systems. Access Systems. Access Systems carried the Sharp copier line as their main line, but also carried Ricoh copiers and Lexmark printers. The company had been in business since 1986. The company was owned by man named Shane Sloan. His VP of Sales was Jon Joint. They were curious about what Toshiba had to offer so they agreed to a meeting with us in 2017. Their focus was to continue to expand their coverage beyond Iowa. They had eleven locations when we started talking with them and were in the process of buying another dealer that would give them a twelfth location. Their problem was that neither of the two manufacturers that they currently carried would expand them to all the markets that they wanted to be in over the next few years. I told them that we were willing to expand them if they hit the market target for the counties, we started with. They wanted assurances from someone higher than the regional level that they could expand to all the areas in their business plan with us. We flew them out to California so that they could meet with our president and vice president.

The meeting went great we agreed to expand them in steps as they hit the targets, and they thought the targets were fair. The bonus with Toshiba was that we also allowed them to count the Lexmark products for their targets. We had several more meetings with them to iron out the details and for Larry White, the VP of Sales, to see their location. This process took about six months. In 2018, Access Systems came on as a Toshiba dealer. We managed to set them up with all the counties that they asked for, which impacted on four of our other dealers marginally. They now cover all of Iowa plus some counties in Nebraska, Minnesota, and Wisconsin. This was to be my last large dealer that I added while at Toshiba, and I can only hope that I made the right decision with this addition. I believe that I did but only time will tell.

In 2019 I was seriously considering retiring. I had not told anyone that I was going to retire, but rumors had begun to circulate. I was always being asked about when I planned to retire by my team and by some of the dealers. I had a resignation letter already written up and on my computer. Out of the blue in early 2020, I received a call from Larry White telling me that Toshiba was going down to three regions and that he knew that I might be considering retiring so he asked me if I wanted to stay and take over one of the three remaining regions or if I was ready to retire. I asked him what the additional territory would encompass. It was a significant amount of additional geography and additional dealers. He also told me that since this was a realignment and that a region would disappear that Toshiba would be offering me a severance package. I had been on the other side of several of these realignments, so I knew exactly how to calculate what the package would be if I elected to retire. He told me to think about it and discuss it with Cindy and get back with him. I discussed it with Cindy, and we ran the numbers. I got back with Larry and picked a date that worked for both sides. He told me to reach out to my team first before the official announcement and let him know when that was completed. I set up a conference call and told my team that I would be retiring and when the date would be. The date was May 1, 2020, and it was about five weeks away. I felt that fate had intervened for me and helped me make the decision to retire a little early. Ironically, this ended up being about four months before the date I was going to tell Toshiba I would be leaving, but because of the restructuring, I ended up with a severance package. If I left on my own, I would have gotten nothing.

Chapter 39
Life After Retirement

Retirement started out as a whirlwind of activity. There were so many decisions that had to be made and things that needed to be finalized with the Toshiba Human Resources department. Once we got past the first three months everything started to calm down. It was exceedingly difficult at first to adapt to not having to race around collaborating with dealers or having conference calls to tell us we were not selling enough products. And of course, Covid was in play at this time, so everything was more complicated. I had started a regular routine of golf, Planet Finess, and various appointments for Cindy and myself. It seemed like we had a full schedule and that things were going ok financially.

All that changed on October 29, 2021. I started my day by going to Top Golf to work on my golf game. It was too cold to go to the golf course that day. I stayed at Top Golf from 10:00 to 12:00 and then came home. We had just ordered a new bed and were going to have the movers take away the old mattress, so I took apart the bed frame upstairs in the bedroom. I suddenly felt a pain shooting down my left leg and yelled down to Cindy that I think I needed to go to the ER. She told me the heck with that I am calling 911. Cindy's decision to call 911 immediately made her the first person to save my life that day. The firehouse is only about two blocks from our house, so they arrived within ten minutes.

By the time the ambulance arrived I was sitting on the floor and had difficulty moving. They did some quick checks of my blood pressure and loaded me into the ambulance and rushed to Delnor Hospital which is only about five miles from our house. Without their speedy arrival, I may not have made it to the hospital. The Batavia paramedics became the second group who saved my life that day. I got to the emergency room and met with the ER doctor his name was Dr. Sinclair. He asked me about where I was having pain, and I told him about the shooting pain in my legs. He ran some tests to see if I had a heart attack, and the results were negative. He diagnosed from my description of the pain and the fact that I did not have a heart attack that my aorta had dissected. He confirmed this with a Cat scan and said, "We need to get him to Northwestern Hospital in downtown Chicago, he needs emergency surgery because his aorta had dissected."

An Aortic dissection is a tearing of the inner walls of the aorta. It causes the blood to rush through the tear and into the middle and outer layers of the aorta. If not treated by surgery in the first twenty-four hours the chances of my survival are minimal. In my case I believe Dr. Sinclair's quick diagnosis that day made him the third person that saved my life that day. They wanted to fly me down by helicopter, but the weather was too bad, so they rushed me down via an ambulance. I do not remember any of the trip downtown, or even the surgery. My only recollection of anything during surgery or shortly thereafter was a negative reaction to one of the drugs they gave me that caused me to believe I was being tortured. I was told by the doctors after the surgery that I had tried to pull the tubes out of my chest, and that I had to be strapped down to keep from hurting myself.

Cindy confirmed what the doctors had told me. I thought I might have just dreamed all of it. The memory of being tied down still haunts me. I was out of it for about four days after the surgery according to those around me. I was told a few things after the fact of what had happened. The actual surgery was to repair a Thoracic Aortic Dissection. They removed about a foot of my aorta and replaced it with a synthetic product. They called the replacement item an elephant's trunk. They also had to check the valve in my heart that was directly attached to the dissection for damages. To do this, they had to stop my heart for part of the procedure. I never found out how long I was dead, but I did not see a light at the end of the tunnel. I do not know if that is good thing or a bad thing, but I do not recall seeing anything. I was told there was no damage to the valve in my heart. The surgery took over ten hours in total. Once I was awake and cognizant of what was going on, I met with my surgeon. His name was Dr. Mehta, he was the fourth person that saved my life that day. Dr. Mehta told Cindy and I that I was incredibly lucky and that if I had not been in such great shape I probably would have died.

I later was told that 90% of those who have a dissection like mine do not survive if surgery is not done in the first twenty-four hours. I started remembering and finding out little items from the surgery from Cindy and my son, Jeff, over the next few days. Things like incubation and feeding tubes. Things I would rather not remember. Jeff stayed with his mother and I while I was in the hospital, which was an immense help for both of us. I was in the hospital for eleven days in total. If I had still been working for Toshiba at the time of my surgery, I probably would have been travelling and been out of state. I could not have had the surgery quickly enough and I would have died. I am sure that God was watching over me on that day. I hope that His being by my side meant that He had things in mind for me in the future.

Chapter 40
Things They Don't Tell You

Everything seemed to go smoothly while I was recovering. I had therapy in a special location in the hospital so that I could be on a monitor while doing the necessary exercises. The initial physical therapy lasted for three months. I then continued a more normal physical therapy for about five more months and was then given the OK to work out a regular gym. I got through the rest of 2022 with no significant issues.

After the first year, I started to have problems with my blood pressure skyrocketing on a few occasions. It happened at times when I was just sitting on the couch and other times I might have been working out. I started to think here we go again I am going to die. I started having panic/anxiety attacks. It got to the point where every little pain made me think that something had gone wrong and that I was going to die. I ended up making several trips to the emergency room.

Each time I went to the Emergency Room, they would run tests and tell me that my heart was ok and that they saw no damage to my aorta. I was physically OK, and I was just having panic attacks. I was then told that I was having a form of PTSD (Post-traumatic stress disorder). Apparently, it is common with people who have had near death experiences. I wish someone had told me about this possible side effect when all of this started. Maybe I could have had some sort of therapy at the beginning and have been better prepared. At that point, I decided that I might need some help if I was ever going to get mentally healthy. I started seeing a psychiatrist and a therapist. I have been seeing them for over a year. It seems to help, but I still do not feel normal. I am not sure that I will ever feel normal again. Now I try to tell myself that I must remember that my life, like all of ours, is in God's hands and I need to accept that reality. I hope that over the next few years that I will have more adventures in my life, but I do not know what God has in store for me or for Cindy. I just need to accept whatever is to come for both of us.

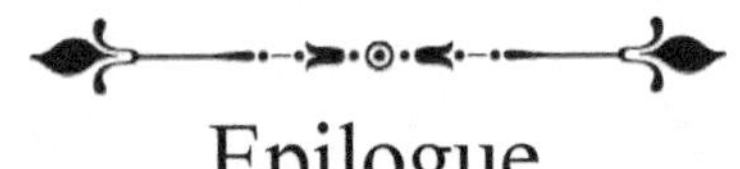

Epilogue

In the meantime, in 2023 big changes came for Toshiba. They were acquired by a Japanese holding company for over two billion dollars. The company that acquired them was named Japanese Industrial Partners. This company has acquired several companies over the years, but this was the largest acquisition to date. Hopefully, this infusion of new money will help Toshiba flourish in the future. This was followed up in 2024 with a second item to impact Toshiba financially. Toshiba Tec announced a merger with Ricoh. The merger is designed to produce machines together, taking advantage of the best practices of each company. The new product lines are scheduled to appear in 2025 for both companies. However, the merger is 85% Ricoh and 15% Toshiba Tec. Knowing this mix I am confident that Ricoh will have the dominant say in what happens next. A comparable situation occurred in 2003 when Konica and Minolta merged. The outcome did not turn out well with Minolta dealers or Minolta management. Toshiba Tec is the parent company of Toshiba America Business Solutions, which is where I was employed. With all the changes at Toshiba, I am extremely glad that I made the decision to retire in 2020.

As I look back on our journey together and the decisions that we made, I am thankful for all the amazing things that Cindy and I have been able to accomplish so far. I am also thankful for all the places we have been able to visit and all the great people we have met along the way. Each of them had their own influence on our lives. As a child I would never have dreamed of what life had in store for us. The most important thing that I have learned in my seventy plus years is that with a little help from God, you can accomplish anything if you set your mind to it. As with all people, there have been difficulties in our lives, but fortunately there have been more ups than downs. I think about all the opportunities that we had to make decisions and how in most cases we chose the right path. My only hope as we enter the twilight of our lives is that God will give us the time to enjoy the fruits of our labor. However, that is a decision that is in His hands to make not ours.